Bringing Mysteries Alive for Children and Young Adults

Jeanette Larson

Linworth
PUBLISHING, INC

Your Trusted
Library-to-Classroom Connection.
Books, Magazines, and Online

Dedication

 This book is dedicated to my mother and father, who introduced me to the great detectives.

Library of Congress Cataloging-in-Publication Data

Larson, Jeanette.
 Bringing mysteries alive for children and young adults / by Jeanette
Larson.
     p. cm.
Includes bibliographical references and index.
 ISBN 1-58683-012-0 (alk. paper)
 1. Children--Books and reading--United States. 2. Teenagers--Books
and reading--United States. 3. Detective and mystery stories--Study and
teaching. 4. Interdisciplinary approach in education. 5. Activity
programs in education. 6. Children's libraries--Activity programs. 7.
Children's literature in series. 8. Children's
literature--Bibliography. I. Title.
Z1037.A1L229 2004
028.5'5--dc22

                        2003022064

Published by Linworth Publishing, Inc.
480 East Wilson Bridge Road, Suite L
Worthington, Ohio 43085

Table of Contents

Preface

Whenever I was asked what I wanted to be when I grew up, I said that I wanted to be a detective. Nancy Drew, and later Ellery Queen, Sherlock Holmes, and Nero Wolfe, lived the most exciting lives I could imagine. I had a burning curiosity to know what was happening in my neighborhood and only narrowly avoided being labeled a snoop. Even today, I want to know the secrets! As a girl reading mysteries, I was able to vicariously live a life of excitement and adventure. I could travel to exotic locations, meet interesting and mysterious people, and be much braver than I have ever been in real life. As fate would have it, I grew up to be a librarian instead of a detective. But I still get to interrogate people, solve puzzles, search for facts, and use clues to determine the truth (okay, it is really a reference interview and I'm helping a library customer) and I still read mysteries to visit exotic places and to safely taste a little danger.

In addition to providing some background on the genre, I have attempted to explain why mysteries are so popular, to define the scope of the genre, and to provide programming ideas and classroom activities that introduce young readers to mysteries. There are many mysteries, including series mysteries, available and I have not included them all. Instead, I have focused on some of my favorites, as well as some that have had lasting interest. I have also included sample titles from some currently popular, but probably ephemeral, series so that teachers and librarians are aware of them. An extensive bibliography provides information about all of the books mentioned in the text. And now, "the game is afoot!"

Acknowledgements

I want to thank my husband, Jim, who also loves mysteries, for his support and assistance. He frequently cleaned the house and cooked the meals so that I could write. He also drew and re-drew patterns and illustrations for this book. I also acknowledge the many wonderful mystery writers whose works have given me many hours of pleasurable reading. Many friends and colleagues, too numerous to name, helped with ideas, suggestions, and books I might have otherwise missed; they know who they are and I thank them. I also thank Carol Simpson, who first accepted this idea for a book, and my editor Donna Miller for her patience and persistence and for knowing when to push and when to hold back.

About the Author

Jeanette Larson is currently the Youth Services Manager for Austin Public Library. Previously she served as the Director of the Library Development Division of the Texas State Library, Public Services Supervisor for Mesquite (TX) Public Library, and as a Children's Librarian at Irving (TX) Public Library. Ms. Larson holds a Master of Science in Library Science from the University of Southern California and a Bachelor of Arts degree from the University of New Mexico. She has worked professionally with children and children's librarians for more than 27 years and has twice served on the Newbery Award Committee. In 1998, the Texas Library Association named her Librarian of the Year.

Her reviews of mystery books have been published in *Mostly Murder* and *School Library Journal*, and she reviews audiobook mysteries for *Booklist*. Jeanette authored *The Secret Code is R*E*A*D*, the manual for the 1990 Texas Reading Club, and has written several articles on using mysteries with children for *Book Links* and other journals. A member of the Heart of Texas Chapter of Sisters in Crime and the Sherlock Holmes Society of Austin, Jeanette's favorite contemporary mystery writers include Mary Willis Walker, Joan Lowery Nixon, Robert Crais, and Robert B. Parker.

Introduction

"Because it is my desire. Is that not enough?" — "The Adventure of the Dancing Detective"

Mysteries are the most popular choice for free selection reading and offer teachers and librarians opportunities to attract reluctant readers, encourage the habit of reading, and challenge outstanding students to stretch their brains. Although mystery is one of the most popular genres, both for children and adults, little coverage is given to mysteries in books that teach about children's literature. Possibly, this is because some scholars like Carol Billman believe that "the mode of mystery is pervasive in children's fiction." She further points out that many popular mainstream children's mysteries are really adventure stories "in which things happen to the protagonist on his or her way to unraveling ... a sequence of surprising events" (Child Reader as Sleuth 31).

By sharing some of my favorite books, helping you find ways to bring mysteries to the kids with whom you work, and providing background and examples of good and great mysteries, I hope that my love of mysteries will be passed along to new readers. As a teacher or librarian, if you are concerned about using mysteries that might be "too scary" or "too realistic," do not use them. Plenty of mysteries focus on solving puzzles, have no bodies or blood, and are mild enough for even the most cautious or conservative person. You know your students, your school, your community, and your library and what is appropriate to use with your groups. It is always best to preview any book or film before using it with a class or group. Individual students may be ready for books that you are not comfortable using with a group. The extensive bibliography in this book will help you find something for any reader.

Many kids enjoy being scared, at least a little bit. James Howe points out that while kids like to be scared, they also like to be reminded that "what's frightening them isn't real." Humor in mysteries allows for feelings of suspense, tension, and fear that are released in a pleasant way. Laughter reminds us "the events ... are not likely to occur in real life" (Mirth 5). Mysteries are a game, games are fun, and kids love games. Therefore, you can successfully combine mystery and humor to introduce some great books to students, even if the stories are a little scary. Children place high importance on suspense, on risk-taking and bravery, and on learning about new locales, so keep these points in mind when selecting books to use with groups of children (7).

The scope of mystery is very broad and this book will include examples from most of the major sub-genres and categories, including true crime, detection, and suspense. While the genre may be called "crime," I have chosen to use the term "mystery." Not all mysteries include a crime, nor are all crime stories mysteries, so the kinder, gentler term will be used in this book since we are working with young people. Whether it is a novel, a puzzle, or a nonfiction book about investigating a crime, if the teacher or librarian can find the right book for the right child, I believe that child will love a mystery. Human nature makes us want to find out what happens! In order to maximize the use of this book and offer a variety of alternatives so that teachers and librarians can select those books, projects, and activities that best suit the needs of their children, a wide range of books is included. Throughout the book, suggestions are offered for additional books that expand the reading selections, Web sites that offer further research, and organizations that can provide additional resources. Whenever possible, the best literature has been included, but books that have current or sustained popularity, regardless of literary quality, are also included.

About the Books

Suggested readings that exemplify the type of mystery are included in the text. Annotations, grade recommendations, and bibliographic data are provided in the Bibliography for all books except the graphic novels mentioned in Chapter 6 and the mystery award-winning books listed in the Appendix. All recommended titles have been positively reviewed, although all are certainly not of equal literary quality. All books, unless otherwise noted, were in print and available for purchase at the time of inclusion.

About Web Sites

All Web sites were current as of publication. Titles and annotations are included for each Web site so that if the URL no longer works, the reader can use a search engine to locate the resource if it still exists. Always check Web sites before sending students to them to ensure that the information is still valid and appropriate!

About the Chapter Quotations

Each chapter begins with a quote from a Sherlock Holmes mystery. They were selected to fit the material about to be presented and, with one exception, as noted, are the words of the master detective. No, it did not take a lot of sleuthing to find them—any teacher or librarian can find many more to use in sharing mysteries in *The Quotable Sherlock Holmes* by John H. Watson, M.D.

Chapter 1

Introducing Mystery

"I have no desire to make mysteries, but it is impossible at the moment of action to enter into long and complex explanations." —"The Adventure of the Dancing Men"

The *Encyclopædia Britannica* defines the detective story as a "type of popular literature dealing with the step-by-step investigation and solution of a crime, usually murder." Traditionally, mystery stories involve an apparently unsolvable puzzle and a detective who uses clues to reach the only logical conclusion. In the interest of fairness to the reader, the solution should be reached using only clues that were legitimately revealed through the story and were available to the reader at the same time they became known to the detective. In this book, we will explore the various types of mysteries and sub-genres that attract young people to reading.

Mysteries will always be a part of life. Beginning with the very source of life there are things we do not know, and things we may never know. Mystery is in our everyday world. Whether it is a missing key, an unexplained phenomenon, or a pet that has disappeared, so many things in life are mysterious!

While mystery has always been a part of the human condition, mystery literature as a recognized genre is relatively new. It could be said that the first murder was committed when Cain killed Abel, and Greek tragedies include mystery and murder. As magistrate, Oedipus had to investigate the murder of his predecessor, not only to solve the crime, but also to ensure his own safety as king.

It was François-Eugène Vidocq who founded the world's first detective bureau in 1817, and so he is accorded the honor as the first "real" detective. Interestingly, Vidocq was first a master criminal, selected to help Napoleon Bonaparte bring order to a crime-ridden Paris. Who knew better how to fight crime than an accomplished criminal? Vidocq's memoirs probably influenced Edgar Allan Poe when he created his fictional detective, C. Auguste Dupin.

The History of Mystery Literature

"The Murders in the Rue Morgue" by Edgar Allan Poe, published in 1841, is considered the first crime story. His short story, "The Tell-Tale Heart," explores guilt and the criminal mind. Many mystery writers pay homage to Poe in their own writing. For example, David A. Adler's detective finds a shopping list hidden in plain sight in *Young Cam Jansen and the Library Mystery*, replicating Poe's "The Purloined Letter."

Following Poe, Wilkie Collins published *The Moonstone* in 1868. Although the detective appears in only a few sections of the story, according to Chris Steinbrunner, Sergeant Cuff is "one of the first and most significant detectives in English literature" (98). The world did not have a full-blown, well-known fictional detective, however, until 1887 when Sir Arthur Conan Doyle wrote *A Study in Scarlet*, featuring Sherlock Holmes. That first book had little effect on the reading public, but when Doyle's second book, *The Sign of Four*, was published in 1890,

reader's thoroughly embraced the exacting, and often exasperating, detective and his sidekick, Dr. John Watson. Today Holmes is undoubtedly one of the most famous literary characters in the world, instantly recognized for his deerstalker hat, distinctive cape, and calabash pipe.

In the 1920s, mystery literature hit its stride. Detectives like Father Brown, Hercule Poirot, Lord Peter Wimsey, and Ellery Queen became household names, and their classic cases still provide popular and scholarly reading. But the 1930s and 1940s are considered to be the golden age of the detective story as Dashiell Hammett, Raymond Chandler, and Ross MacDonald wrote stories about hard-boiled American private eyes, Erle Stanley Gardner chronicled the trials of Perry Mason, and John Le Carre added spies and espionage to the genre.

Figure 1.1: Sherlock Holmes silhouette

With so much going on in the adult publishing world, it is not surprising that writers would look to children's books. German writer Erich Kästner is recognized as the author of the first children's detective story, *Emil and the Detectives*, published in 1929. However, the Nancy Drew and Hardy Boys mysteries gave the genre its biggest boost because of their phenomenal sales and widespread availability. Many of these early mysteries were very formulaic and featured kids who stumbled upon a crime to solve. *Harriet the Spy* by Louise Fitzhugh, published in 1964, is the first children's book to feature a character that considers herself a professional detective.

The Mystery Writers of America began recognizing quality in children's mysteries in 1961 when they awarded the first Edgar Award for juvenile mystery to Phyllis Whitney for *The Mystery of the Haunted Pool*. But mysteries written for children failed to attract much critical attention until *The Westing Game* by Ellen Raskin won the 1979 Newbery Award.

Why Mysteries Appeal to Readers

Ellery Queen called mysteries "fairy tales for grown-ups" and the same can be said about mysteries for young readers. Carol Billman concludes, "Series like Nancy Drew pick up where fairy tales ... typically leave off" (Child Reader as Sleuth 39) and Michael O. Tunnell speculates that it is the "gaming spirit that exudes from mystery stories" that makes them so popular with young readers (242). In spite of predictions by children's literature specialists that the popularity of mysteries would quickly fade, interest has not waned. In *Through the Eyes of A Child: An*

Introduction to Children's Literature, Donna Norton summarizes research that indicates that children identified mysteries as their top reading preference (47% of average readers and 43% of gifted readers selected mysteries over other genres) (105). But Tunnell says it best: "Fifty years of children's reading preference studies clearly indicate that mystery stories have long been of primary interest to young readers" (242).

Many people are fascinated by mysteries and are attracted to the unknown. Many readers enjoy puzzles and appreciate a clever plot, a timely twist, and attention to the details. Moreover, when we are not ourselves in jeopardy, some of us even enjoy a touch of danger. Mysteries are escape literature. The reader has to actively participate in the story, so mysteries provide mental gymnastics, the spirit of adventure, and vicarious thrills. They offer a game where justice prevails and the world is re-established to an even keel. Often, mysteries, like *Phoning a Dead Man* by Gillian Cross, take us to exotic settings and foreign locales. Perhaps most importantly, they provide us with the feeling of being in control.

The development of "higher order" thinking skills has become increasingly important to the education process. Students must be able to read material or listen to a speech and evaluate the information provided in order to draw their own conclusions. Mysteries offer opportunities to develop problem-solving skills. Detectives, whether fictional or real, use observation, brainpower, thoughtful analysis, a healthy dose of skepticism, and an understanding of human nature more often than they use weapons or muscle. They are problem-solvers who use research, scientific principles, logic, and analysis to put together the evidence and build a case against the criminal.

Informal surveys that regularly appear on DorothyL, an Internet mystery discussion list <http://www.dorothyl.com>, indicate that most of the lifelong readers in the group attribute their love of reading as adults to having read mysteries, and series mysteries in particular, as children. Author Joan Lowery Nixon frequently spoke about otherwise reluctant readers who read one of her books and then asked for another mystery.

Mysteries also provide social, cultural, and historical perspective, both of the time and society in which they were written and of the time and society in which they are set. Readers learn about Victorian London through Sir Arthur Conan Doyle's Sherlock Holmes stories, discover the world of Ancient Rome through Henry Winterfeld's *Detectives in Togas,* and develop an appreciation for our national parks and ecology through the National Parks Mystery series written by Gloria Skurzynski and Alane Ferguson.

Mystery writers, like Willo Davis Roberts, also point out that mystery books require "good characterization, fast-moving plot, entertaining and credible dialogue, and a satisfying resolution" (23). In order to hold the reader's interest, the mystery has to start with a hook and grab the reader into the story. The suspense has to be maintained until the very end. These elements encourage young people to keep reading and to want to read another!

Unlike the content of adult books, cultural diversity has not made great inroads into mysteries for young people. In adult mysteries, we find detectives who are African-American, Hispanic, Native American, and Asian, as well as gay and lesbian detectives. With just a few notable exceptions, most detectives in children's mysteries are still Anglo or animal. Additionally, there are almost no writers of color creating mysteries for kids. In searching for mystery writers of color, one can find some authors who have written a few mysteries among their other works. Virginia Hamilton won the Edgar Award for *The House of Dies Drear,* but she did not, apparently, consider herself a mystery writer. With six mysteries published, and a sequel to *The Spray-Paint Mystery* in the works, Angela Shelf Medearis is among the most prolific African-American writers of mysteries. There are few Hispanic mystery writers for children, and

Rodney Johnson, who has written two mysteries that feature a Lakota sleuth, and Laurence Yep stand almost alone representing diversity in series mysteries for children.

African-American Mysteries

- *Carlotta's Secret* by Patricia E. Canterbury.
- *Circle of Fire* by Evelyn Coleman.
- *Ernestine and Amanda: Mysteries on Monroe Street* by Sandra Belton.
- *Smiffy Blue: Ace Crime Detective* by Walter Dean Myers.

Violence and Mystery Readers

There are three basic values in mystery literature: good wins and evil is punished; brains are better than brawn; life is sacred (Flack xvi). Consider these values if you are concerned that mysteries contain too much violence for young readers. In reality, there is very little violence in most mysteries for young people (and almost never in books for very young readers), and good always prevails. Ethics and morality are interwoven into most mysteries. Criminals are generally portrayed as less intelligent, prone to committing acts of stupidity, and they are usually caught!

Willo Davis Roberts was one of the first writers to alter the tradition of non-violent mysteries for children with her 1975 book *The View From the Cherry Tree* in which an 11-year-old boy witnesses a murder. Although Roberts points out that many authors of mysteries for children use "crimes that are not major felonies" for their plots, she usually involves her characters in kidnapping, murder, extortion, and money laundering. For doing this, Roberts says she has been criticized, "but almost never by the young readers" (23). How the author handles the crime means more in the final analysis than what crime is actually used and most young readers will not read about something that they are not ready to handle. Books such as *Killing Mr. Griffith* by Lois Duncan and *The Face on the Milk Carton* by Caroline Cooney are frequently subjected to challenges for being in library collections. Recent young adult books like Robert Cormier's *The Rag and Bone Shop* deal with tough issues, but also offer a springboard for discussion.

Parents and other adults often express concern about books that portray violence and criminal activities. Concerns about violence, and the role mystery literature can play in raising awareness about crime, ethics, morality, and criminality, will be explored in Chapter 3.

Chapter 2

Defining Mystery

"There are difficulties; there are certainly difficulties." —"The Sign Of Four"

Mystery, detective story, suspense, thriller, puzzler, crime story. What do these words mean? Are they synonymous terms or variations of the genre? Are there differences between a mystery and a detective story? What about horror and suspense? Do we include them in the genre? Ultimately, do the nuances of semantics matter to the reader? Carol Billman calls mysteries a "supergenre" because they intertwine other kinds of fiction, and the flexibility of mysteries for young people lends to the genre the ability to appeal to a wide range of readers (The Child Reader as Sleuth 40). Therefore, many books that may not be pure mystery can appropriately be assigned to the genre, but we will explore some specific definitions.

Mysteries usually involve a crime, sometimes include a dead body or a missing person, and generally focus on a detective or an amateur investigator who must seek a solution to the puzzle. The term suspense can be used to describe almost any story that keeps the reader on the edge of his or her seat. Many suspense books involve a mystery or the need to solve a puzzle in order to resolve the suspense and allow a return to normalcy. Horror stories can include a mystery, especially if the protagonist is trying to discover the source of the horror. Gothic horror, usually involving a haunting or terror, is included in this book if the haunting is related to a mystery.

Types of Mysteries

There are almost as many types of mysteries as there are writers. In fact, some writers chafe at being classified as a mystery writer, believing that it limits their readership to mystery fans. Others write books for a general readership, but if the book contains a mystery, it may be categorized as such by a segment of the reading audience. Mystery readers, whether adult or child, specifically seek out mysteries and want them to be broadly classified as such in libraries and bookstores, but frequently we also want to read a specific sub-genre that narrows our focus to the type of mystery we most enjoy.

There is no definitive listing of sub-genres, but some of the more commonly recognized ones are described here, with examples of titles for young people that fit the category. As always among mystery readers, some may quibble with the placement of a title in one category rather than another, and nuances of the genre might allow a title to be placed on multiple lists.

Cozies (Traditional Mysteries)

Cozy is a descriptor typically used for the classic or traditional mystery. The roots of the cozy are based in Great Britain. Traditionally, the story was set in an old English manor house, but today the mystery can take place anywhere. Increasingly the term is also being used to refer to any mystery that is bloodless, although a murder and a body may be included in the story.

In its purest form, the cozy is a mystery set in a small community, which can be a town or village or any group of people with common interests. A limited number of people could have committed the crime. An amateur investigator, who is frequently considered the town busy-body, generally solves the mystery. Although there are a few notable exceptions, in adult mysteries, cozies have come to be an almost exclusively female sub-genre with the books written by women and the lead characters usually female.

Typically, the suspects are part of a closed group—members of a family, a village, folks at a party—and the amateur detective uses careful observation, an understanding of human nature, and knowledge of local gossip and scandal to deduce the solution. Cozies often adhere to an unstated set of rules that ensure fair play for the reader. Agatha Christie's Miss Marple books are cozies, and mystery fans can easily find a modern example of the cozy mystery by watching the television show, "Murder She Wrote."

Within children's publishing, there are traditional mysteries available for even the youngest readers. A book like *Max and Molly and the Mystery of the Missing Honey* by Jürg Obrist offers beginning readers the opportunity to solve a simple crime. Most of Agatha Christie's writing is suitable for young adult readers, but they may also enjoy the Cat series by Lilian Jackson Braun, the Mrs. Pollifax books by Dorothy Gilman, and Nancy Atherton's Aunt Dimity series.

> ***Suggested Books—Cozies:***
> *The Callender Papers* by Cynthia Voigt.
> *Gus and Gertie and the Missing Pearl* by Joan Lowery Nixon.
> *Piggins* by Jane Yolen.
> *Two Miss Mallard Mysteries* by Robert Quackenbush.

Amateur Sleuths

Literally, anyone can be an amateur sleuth and this is one of the largest categories of mystery. A popular amateur sleuth is the person who enjoys solving a mystery, but does not particularly seek out cases to solve. This would include Nancy Drew, the Hardy Boys, the Three Investigators, and Miss Mallard, the famous duck-tective. Unlike a few exceptions in adult mysteries in which the investigator is a cat or an alien, the detectives in children's books do not have to be human. Even the very youngest readers will find many examples to choose from, as many of the mysteries written for children utilize an amateur detective.

The amateur detective appeals to many readers because he or she is someone like us—an ordinary person of reasonable intelligence who relies on his or her abilities to observe, apply reason, and be persistent. Additionally, once the case is solved, the amateur detective returns to a regular life that is quiet and relatively normal except when he or she stumbles onto a case. In fact, sometimes the skills and training that the amateur detective uses in his or her real life are the skills that help solve the case.

> **Suggested Books—Amateur Sleuths:**
> *Adventure in Wyoming: X Country Adventures* by Bob Schaller.
> *The Berenstain Bear Scouts and the Missing Merit Badge Mystery*
>   by Stan Berenstain.
> *The Case of the Wiggling Wig* by E.W. Hildick.
> *Kidnap at the Catfish Café* by Patricia Reilly Giff.
> *Vancouver Nightmare: A Tom Austen Mystery* by Eric Wilson.

Accidental Investigators

While some amateur detectives regularly take on cases, another type of sleuth is the "accidental" investigator. This is someone who because of circumstances ends up investigating and solving one crime, and who probably never encounters another mystery. These books are usually single titles since once the detective begins to solve cases on a regular basis he or she becomes an amateur detective. Most of Joan Lowery Nixon's young adult books involve accidental detectives. The accidental detective is appealing because it allows the reader to vicariously enjoy the excitement of a mystery, while recognizing that these things don't really happen to most of us on a regular basis. It is intriguing to think that a common person going about his or her daily business might help to solve a crime.

> **Suggested Books—Accidental Investigators:**
> *Close to a Killer* by Marsha Qualey.
> *The Pet-sitting Peril* by Willo Davis Roberts.
> *The Secret of Gumbo Grove* by Eleanor Tate.
> *Spy Cat* by Peg Kehret.
> *Who Are You?* by Joan Lowery Nixon.

Professional Sleuths

Professional detectives solve crimes or locate people or possessions for a living. They work regularly at their job and are paid for their efforts. Professional crime solvers may be public servants, like police officers and agents of the government, or private detectives who are in business for themselves. The professional detective appeals to readers who enjoy the details of criminal investigation because the books usually allow us to learn police procedure, techniques of investigation, and the science of sleuthing. Many young people who are interested in careers in law enforcement or criminal justice may also enjoy nonfiction books that involve professional crime solving.

Private Investigators

Private investigators work for a fee and are loyal to the client who hired them. Private eye novels can be hard-boiled, usually defined by the level of violence, rough language, and toughness, or soft-boiled, featuring a kinder, gentler detective. The emphasis in most private investigator mysteries is on the personality of the detective rather than on the process he or she uses to solve the crime. The private investigators can usually employ techniques that are not available to the police or other professional investigators since they do not have to follow all of the rules of the legal system. They frequently work by simply staying in the background and observing, talking to unsuspecting people, and surreptitiously gathering clues. Of course, the private investigator also does not have the powers or protection enjoyed by the police and other officials.

In mysteries for children, the private investigator may be a child or an animal. Unlike the amateur detective, who stumbles onto the case, the private investigator solves crimes as a vocation, in a deliberate manner, seeking out cases. Even in mysteries for children, the private investigator usually has an office or a place of business and regular hours and is compensated for solving the case. Because it is unlikely that a crime spree will occur in any single location, authors of series that feature an amateur detective must often look for ways to move the protagonist to new locations or to bring new cases into the community.

Hard-boiled mysteries are uniquely American in origin. They are the classic private eye mysteries that feature a tough guy (or beginning in the late-1970s, a tough woman) detective. The private eye is usually a loner (although an assistant or side-kick may be available) with his or her own code of ethics, and sometimes a commitment to social consciousness. Often the private detective is taking cases that the police cannot or will not pursue, so the client is frequently viewed as the underdog, someone for whom there would otherwise be no justice.

Books for children can maintain the flavor of Raymond Chandler's "mean streets." The writing in hard-boiled private eye books often contains a layer of sarcastic humor, lowbrow wit, or double entendre. While most of the adult books of this type are not appropriate for young readers, their influence on the genre can be seen in many books written for kids. Bruce Hale's Chet Gecko series pays homage to the wit of Chandler and other writers from the golden age of mysteries. The humor and wit appeal to young readers even though they may not comprehend the allusions to the works of other writers.

The professional private investigator frequently appears to have no personal life. The reader rarely knows much about what the detective does when he or she is "off duty." The sub-genre began with the writings of Chandler and Hammett but continues today in adult mysteries by Robert Parker, Robert Crais, and Sue Grafton. Although they are children, Encyclopedia Brown and Cam Jansen are professional detectives because they work cases on a regular basis. Picture books, like *Sheep in Wolves' Clothing* by Staoshi Kitamura, may introduce the concept of a detective who is asked to help solve a problem.

Suggested Books—Private Investigators:
High-Rise Private Eye: The Case of the Missing Monkey by Cynthia Rylant.
Inspector Hopper by Doug Cushman.
Jake Gander, Storyville Detective: The Case of the Greedy Granny
    by George McClements.
Kid Caramel Private Investigator: The Case of the Missing Ankh
    by Dwayne J. Ferguson.
Private I. Guana: The Case of the Missing Chameleon by Nina Laden.

Police Procedurals

Official investigators have the power of law behind them and readers who want "just the facts" are drawn to police stories. Nonfiction books that allow the reader to learn how the criminal justice system works and how investigators solve real-life crimes fit this sub-genre. Court procedure books, like *The O.J. Simpson Trial: What It Shows Us About Our Legal System* by Nathan Aaseng, follow the police investigation and subsequent trials of infamous people.

Even in works of fiction, police departments do not allow children to participate in investigations, so there are few true examples of police procedurals for children. Books like *Officer Buckle and Gloria* by Peggy Rathman show police officers at work and Alison Hart's Police Story books allow young readers to ride along with police officers in a manner similar to some reality television shows.

Many mystery novels written for kids do include details of police work, however, so those looking for aspects of police procedurals will find them in many of the books by Joan Lowery Nixon and others. Robert Cormier's novel *The Rag and Bone Shop* provides a very real look at police interrogation techniques. Teachers might also include nonfiction books about the legal profession as a career and biographies of lawyers, as well as fictional books that feature lawyers.

Suggested Books—Police Procedures:
Andy Russell NOT Wanted by the Police by David A. Adler.
Chase: A Police Story by Alison Hart.
Cop on the Beat: Officer Steven Mayfield in New York City
    by Arelene Schulman.
The Dark Stairs by Betsy Byars.
Detective Dinosaur Lost and Found by James Skofield.

Historical Mystery

Historical fiction has increased in popularity in recent years so it is not surprising to find that more historical mysteries are being written. The writer has to know enough about the period to ensure a sense of authenticity. The processes used to solve the crime must be accurate for the time. For example, fingerprinting only came into use as a detection tool in the early part of the 20th century, so it cannot be used in Winterfeld's *Detectives in Togas*.

Readers who enjoy history are particularly appreciative of the information that can be gained from an historical mystery, but the writer must balance the amount of historical information provided so that it does not overpower the mystery. Historical mysteries also allow the author to bring in real-life historical characters, such as Avi does in *The Man Who was Poe*, which includes Edgar Allan Poe as a character, or *The Mark Twain Murders* by Laurence Yep. Historical mystery is also popular because the author can investigate mysteries that would seem too simple in today's fast-paced society. Additionally, historical settings may allow for less violent crimes to be committed and for the author to explore a time when social mores were different.

A popular sub-set of historical mystery is the time travel mystery, wherein the protagonist is transported to another time, and either solves a mystery while in the past or needs information from the past to solve a contemporary problem. Often the plot's twists and turns are dictated by the protagonist's efforts to alter personal or family history, to change the outcome of history, or to thwart disaster or stop a crime. Kathryn Reiss has written several excellent books that combine modern and historical mysteries through time travel, including *Paperquake: a Puzzle*, set in San Francisco. One of the most masterful time travel mysteries is *Mr. Was* by Pete Hautman; the sophisticated plot combines time travel with attempted murder, family secrets, and an almost perfect crime.

Keep in mind that what is historical to a child may be only a few generations back to an adult. While many historical mysteries take place before the 20th century, the period can be as late as the 1970s or 1980s. Mysteries that were written in a previous era are not considered to be historical mysteries simply because they take place during that time. For example, Sir Arthur Conan Doyle was writing about his own time, so the Sherlock Holmes stories are not historical mysteries.

> **Suggested Books—Historical Mystery:**
> *The December Rose* by Leon Garfield.
> *The Golden Goblet* by Eloise McGraw.
> *Mystery of the Dark Tower* by Evelyn Coleman.
> *Secret in St. Something* by Barbara Brooks Wallace.
> *The Thieves of Ostia* by Caroline Lawrence.

Person in Jeopardy

In the world of adult mysteries, this category is called "Woman in Jeopardy" because the stories usually involve a "damsel" in distress. There is also a sub-category where children are in danger, and because this strikes a bit too close to real life, some adult mystery readers are adamant about not reading those books. In most juvenile mysteries it is a child who is in danger, and only rarely an adult, so the author has labeled this category with the broader term "person" in jeopardy. Avi's *Wolf Rider* is a notable example of this sub-category that usually involves an innocent person who is caught in the middle of a crime. A stranger's confession that he has committed a murder puts a young boy's life in danger.

Other books that fit this sub-genre might involve a kidnapping, a missing child, or a young person who is put into a dangerous situation because of a parent's employment or action. Joan Lowery Nixon's books provide several examples of this situation, as does *Don't Look Behind You* by Lois Duncan, where April's life is endangered after her father testifies at a trial. In *Locked Inside* by Nancy Werlin, a teenage girl is kidnapped and her computer role-playing games may be her salvation.

> **Suggested Books—Person in Jeopardy:**
> *Are You in the House Alone?* by Richard Peck.
> *Coffin on a Case* by Eve Bunting.
> *Counterfeit Son* by Elaine Marie Alphin.
> *Don't Tell Anyone* by Peg Kehret.
> *The Man in the Woods* by Rosemary Wells.

Ghosts and Gothic

Ghost stories, tales of the supernatural, horror, and other stories about apparitions are where mystery and fantasy intersect. Because they often contain a mystery (Who is haunting the house and why? What is the ghost trying to tell us?), some ghost stories are included in this book. Ghost stories often take place in old houses or in a new building that has been constructed on the site where something terrible happened years earlier.

Ghost stories often allow the reader to get a taste of history and may also include time travel. Books like *There's a Dead Person Following My Sister Around* by Vivian Vande Velde and *House of Dies Drear* by Virginia Hamilton take the reader to another era and, as with historical mysteries, can easily be integrated into history lessons or programs.

Often the mystery takes place in a building with a secret room or hidden passage. Examples include *Up from Jericho Tel* by E.L. Konigsburg, most books by John Bellairs, and many of Betty Ren Wright's novels. These books can take place in an historical setting or, like *The Ghost Sitter* by Peni Griffin, intertwine contemporary settings with ghostly mysteries from the past. Sometimes the ghost is not even human. *Ghost Dog* by Ellen Leroe has an invisible pug helping to solve the mystery of a stolen baseball card.

> ***Suggested Books—Ghosts and Gothic:***
> *Billy the Ghost and Me* by Gery Gree and Rob Ruddick.
> *Down a Dark Hall* by Lois Duncan.
> *Meg Mackintosh and the Mystery at Camp Creepy* by Lucinda Landon.
> *Something Upstairs: a Tale of Ghosts* by Avi.
> *Stonewords: a Ghost Story* by Pam Conrad.

Suspense

In suspense novels, we are scared by our own imagination and a real or perceived sense of what is "lurking around the corner." Often the culprit is identified early in the story, and suspense is generated through the uncertainty of the outcome—can the protagonist outwit the villain? Frequently there is also a race against time or a chase involved in the story. Can the protagonist get help in time or can he or she outrun the villain to escape and get help? One of the most chilling suspense novels for young people is *The Girl in the Box* by Ouida Sebestyen. A young girl is left in an underground cement room and does not know when, or even if, her captor will return.

This sub-genre can be thought of as having a "boo!" factor. Events occur, leading toward a "gotcha" outcome. On a very basic level, books for young children such as *A Dark, Dark Tale* by Ruth Brown, *The Ghost of Sifty-Sifty Sam* by Angela Shelf Medearis, and *The Tailypo!* by Joanna Galdone are suspense. Suitable for preschool read-aloud, these books introduce youngsters to the sub-genre, and adults can add to the suspense by modulating their reading voice between whispers and shouts.

Some readers divide suspense into thrillers and horror. Horror can include realistic horror or supernatural horror, such as vampires and malevolent spirits. Elements of fear, rather than curiosity, also distinguish suspense from gothic mystery, where the protagonist is usually not fearful of the spirits, but is helping to resolve a mystery so that the ghost can rest. Clearly there are books that could be categorized in multiple sub-genres. Mysteries that involve the supernatural (*The Dollhouse Murders* by Betty Ren Wright, for example) are included in this book.

> ***Suggested Books—Suspense:***
> *Don't Scream* by Joan Lowery Nixon.
> *Megan's Island* by Willo Davis Roberts.
> *Skeleton Man* by Joseph Bruchac.
> *Tightrope* by Gillian Cross.
> *What Became of Her?* by M.E. Kerr.

Locked Room Mysteries

Locked room mysteries are a type of suspense novel. They usually involve a seemingly impossible situation, e.g., a body is found in a room that was locked, secured from within, or had no unobservable means of egress available. Although it appears to be impossible, the mystery is, in fact, readily solvable through careful observation and logic. While some of these mysteries literally occur in a locked room, the sub-genre includes examples set on islands, in remote locations, or in some other closed environment (for example, a train) where the number of potential suspects is limited, but the case appears to have no solution. The sub-group can also include puzzlers or mysteries that involve solving a puzzle in order to resolve the problem.

Edgar Allan Poe introduced the first locked room mystery in his 1841 story, "The Murders in the Rue Morgue." Agatha Christie's classic *Murder on the Orient Express* and "The Problem of Cell 13" by Jacque Futrelle are archetypal examples of the sub-genre. Sherlock Holmes says it best when he points out in *The Sign of Four* that "when you have eliminated the impossible, whatever remains, however improbable, must be the truth." Often booby traps, secret passages, or another trick is the key to the solution. Locked room mysteries tend to be more complicated and usually focus more on the puzzle and less on the characters and story.

Ellen Raskin's *The Westing Game* is probably the best-known locked room mystery written specifically for young readers. Sixteen people must solve a puzzle to claim their inheritance, if they can survive. Another mystery specifically written for children that includes a locked room mystery is Avi's *The Man Who Was Poe*. Edmund is searching for his mother and meets Mr. Dupin (Poe) who helps solve a locked room mystery when his sister also disappears. On a more contemporary note, *Alien Secrets* by Annette Curtis Klause takes place on a space ship. A dead body is found on board and everyone is a suspect!

> ***Suggested Books—Locked Room Mysteries:***
> *The Eleventh Hour* by Graeme Base.
> *The Emperor and the Kite* by Jane Yolen.
> *Meg Mackintosh and the Mystery in the Locked Library* by Lucinda Landon.
> *The Name of the Game was Murder* by Joan Lowery Nixon.

Espionage and Spies

Secrets, betrayal, the romance of James Bond, double dealing, disguises, and exotic travel combine to make spy novels and techno-thrillers popular. In children's books, the spy is not usually going after big government or underworld gangs that are trying to take over the world. Rather the spying is more localized and generally confined to the neighborhood. *Harriet the Spy* is one of the most well-known examples of this sub-genre.

Part of the attraction for movies like *Spy Kids* and *Mission Impossible*, or those featuring James Bond and Austin Powers, is the amazing assortment of high-tech weapons, transportation, and tools available to the secret agents. Because kids, especially boys, love technology, techno-thrillers can be included in this category even if they are not truly spy novels. As would be expected, more books that include the use of the Internet, fancy gadgets, and even science fiction inspired transportation are being written for kids today. Of course, not every mystery that features the Internet is a techno-thriller. *Crusader* by Edward Bloor involves a virtual reality game in the search for the murderer of a teenager's mother but has nothing to do with spies and espionage.

This category can also be used to introduce nonfiction books related to espionage, secret codes, and historical spies and traitors. Books like *The Code Book: How to Make It, Break It, Hack It, Crack It* by Simon Singh provide hours of enjoyable (and informational) reading for fans of cryptography. *Spy Satellites* by Paul Kupperberg provides a look at the technology of espionage. For younger children, use books like *Each Peach Pear Plum* by Janet Ahlberg or *I Spy Mystery: a Book of Picture Riddles* by Jane Marzollo to begin honing powers of observation and developing investigator skills.

Suggested Books—Fiction—Espionage and Spies:
Adam Sharp: London Calling by George Edward Stanley.
Howie Bowles, Secret Agent by Kate Banks.
Mara, Daughter of the Nile by Eloise Jarvis McGraw.
Owen Foote, Super Spy by Stephanie Greene.
Stormbreaker by Anthony Horowitz.

Suggested Books—Nonfiction—Espionage and Spies:
The Amazing Life of Moe Berg: Catcher, Scholar, Spy
　　by Tricia Andryszewski.
Spying: The Modern World of Espionage by Ron Fridell.
Traitor: The Case of Benedict Arnold by Jean Fritz.
The Ultimate Spy Book by H. Keith Melton.
Unsung Heroes of World War II: The Story of the Navajo Code Talkers
　　by Deanne Durrett.

True Crime

True crime in the world of adult mysteries includes factual reconstruction of a crime and the courtroom proceedings. Although the reader usually already knows the outcome of the case, true crime aficionados appreciate reading about the details that lead to justice. Many true crime readers are fascinated by the boundaries of human behavior and want to know how someone can commit what is usually a very heinous and inhumane crime. The sub-genre also includes nonfiction books about pirates, like *Terror of the Spanish Main: Sir Henry Morgan and His Buccaneers* by Albert Marrina, which are very popular reading choices for some children.

As with many adult books, some novels for young people use a true crime or mystery as the basis for the story. The fictionalized account may allow the author to hypothesize about an unsolved crime, add a touch of realism to a fictional story, or explore issues in a manner that is appropriate for young readers. *Mississippi Trial, 1955* by Chris Crowe is a fictionalized exploration of the murder of a black teenager, Emmett Till. Crowe tells the story from the point of view of a white teenager visiting his grandfather in Mississippi. Pair this novel with Crowe's nonfiction examination of the case, *Getting Away With Murder: The True Story of the Emmett Till Case*. *A Northern Light* by Jennifer Donnelly uses the Chester Gillette case, which was the basis for Theodore Dreiser's novel,

An American Tragedy, and the film *A Place in the Sun*, as the backdrop for a coming-of-age tale and murder mystery.

Teenage readers may be attracted to adult true crime books, but most true crime that is specifically written for children explores historical figures, like Allen Pinkerton, Al Capone, or Jesse James, or offers a look at crime fighting techniques and the science of criminal investigations. The books are often written specifically for the school and library market, so they take into account the need for less graphic description of crimes. Titles like *Simon Wiesenthal: Tracking Down Nazi Criminals* by Laura S. Jeffery can be used to explore history and to show that research and careful note taking can be used to capture criminals.

While true crime books written for kids generally do not include a lot of the lurid details of murders or Mafia hits found in many adult books, some young people will find true crime to be fascinating. Prudent teachers and librarians will probably not offer true crime books except in response to specific requests, but we should not be overly concerned about teens and pre-teens who seek them. Most kids will not read books they are not able to handle and several studies have demonstrated that we do not need to be overly concerned about kids who are reading, even if they are reading somewhat gory books.

For young people, this category includes a fascinating array of books about forensic science, crime scene investigation, police work, accounts of trials, and biographies of famous criminals and detectives. Use books like *When Objects Talk: Solving a Crime with Science* by Mark Friedlander, Jr., to help students understand the scientific methods behind criminal investigation.

Some true crime titles can help young people understand the harsh realities of a "life of crime" and, hopefully, dissuade them from making inappropriate choices. Jack Gantos' masterful autobiography, *A Hole in My Life*, clearly shows the misery, and potential horror, that befalls a young man who was incarcerated for smuggling drugs. This book has been particularly useful for teachers and librarians who work with youth in the juvenile justice system because it also clearly demonstrates that a person can overcome adversity, embrace rehabilitation, and lead a productive adult life. Other books that offer a powerful point for teens who may need a dose of reality include *Life in Prison* by Stanley "Tookie" William (co-founder of the Crips gang) and *We're Not Monsters: Teens Speak Out about Teens in Trouble* by Sabrina Solin Weill.

Suggested Books—Younger Readers—True Crime:
Case Closed: the Real Scoop on Detective Work by Milton Meltzer.
Crimebusters: The Investigation of Murder by Brian Lane.
DNA Fingerprinting: The Ultimate Identity by Ron Fridell.
Fingerprints and Talking Bones: How Real-Life Crimes are Solved
   by Charlotte Jones.
Sensational Trials of the 20th Century by Betsy Harvey Kraft.

Suggested Books—Young Adults—True Crime:
Gangsters by Gary L. Blackwood.
Kids Who Kill by Herma Silverstein.
Serial Killers by Louise Gerdes.
The Trial of Charles Manson: California Cult Murders by Bradley Steffens.
Who Killed My Daughter? by Lois Duncan.

Chapter 3

Appreciating Mysteries

"There's plenty of thread, no doubt, but I can't get the end of it into my hand. Now, I'll state the case clearly and concisely, and maybe you can see a spark where all is dark to me." —"The Man with the Twisted Lip"

Children enjoy mysteries because they are curious about the world around them. The unknown often intrigues mystery readers. Mysteries do not have to be scary, and do not even have to involve a crime. In most mysteries written for young people, the child is empowered to solve problems, be the hero, take risks, and help others.

Joan Lowery Nixon, four-time Edgar award winning author, said it best—"kids love a mystery!" Nixon often related the story of a 14-year-old girl who had, by her own admission, never read a book all the way to the end. That is, the child told Nixon, until a friend shared a copy of *The Stalker* with her. "I loved it," the girl told Nixon. "I've read every mystery you've ever written and mysteries other authors have written. Mysteries are the way to go." The young girl then thanked Nixon for the gift of reading (Mystery Writers of America).

The Power of Mysteries

Often the key to reaching reluctant readers is to help them find something that interests them, that suits their taste, and that is engaging yet accessible. Michael O. Tunnell describes the process a good writer uses as tossing "the gauntlet" before the reader. The gaming spirit prevalent in mysteries is the power that draws "children to the world of books and literacy" (242). Carol Billman points out that mysteries have an "implicit command to readers to participate in the guessing game of detection" ("The Child Reader as Sleuth" 30). Young readers are engaged in the story and in the puzzle. *Becoming a Nation of Readers*, a study led by Dr. Richard C. Anderson for the U.S. Department of Education, concluded that the key to a student's reading is interest in the material, which far outweighs its readability level. Every librarian and teacher has worked with a young person who, when inspired by the right book and motivated by personal desire, has read material that far exceeded the child's usual ability.

In discussing all young readers, Tunnell states that "Mysteries vicariously fill the need, especially in an adolescent, to become a competent, self-sufficient, and productive individual. The young protagonists in mystery stories ... take their courage in hand and, against all odds, come out on top. Good problem solvers and detectives are bloodhounds for facts and clues. They are systematic" (244). We certainly want to teach children to be competent and self-sufficient and good research skills require that children sort through clues, systematically hunt for answers, and solve problems.

Rite of Passage

Given all the problems young people face today, it is also legitimate for adults to wonder why children might purposefully frighten themselves by reading about crime, violence, death, and fear. Not every mystery includes these elements, but, especially in books for older children, many do. Some researchers believe that this attraction to danger is part of growing up, a rite of passage similar to those practiced in tribal societies. Ritual or symbolic danger is used to represent real, albeit hopefully rare, threats. The conflicts that young people face in mystery novels reflect the popular culture and realities of contemporary life. Mystery literature creates an environment where the reader can face and overcome danger and, along with the protagonist, be brave enough to address the conflict, resolve the problem, gain control of the situation, and prevail.

Moral Behavior

Mysteries are generally very moral. Good wins, justice prevails, and society's values are upheld; crime is shown as wrong and the perpetrator is punished. Because right and wrong are explicitly described in mysteries, the moral lessons are obvious and understandable. Thus, mysteries provide many opportunities to expand a young person's understanding of approved mores and codes of conduct and concepts of appropriate and inappropriate behavior, and to develop empathy for those who are wronged or injured by the actions of criminals or wrongdoers.

Challenging Gifted Students

Jerry D. Flack encourages teachers to use mysteries with all readers, but especially with gifted students. At a very basic level, the vocabulary can be challenging, especially in the classic novels of Agatha Christie, Raymond Chandler, Dorothy L. Sayers, and Wilkie Collins, and the plots complex enough to provide gifted students with a demanding reading experience (xvii). On a higher level, mysteries also provide opportunities for research, interdisciplinary studies, thought provoking discussion, and intelligent role models. Mysteries encourage students to read critically, pay attention to details, think logically, draw conclusions, and solve problems.

Class Discussion: Mystery fiction often depicts the culture of the times in which the stories were written. Race relations, gender roles, politics, and technology influence the story and reflect contemporary mores. Read a short story by Edgar Allan Poe, Sir Arthur Conan Doyle, Rex Stout, or another author. Ask these questions:

- From the story, what can we determine about the community?
- What modes of transportation were used?
- What are some of the slang words used then that are no longer heard today?
- Is the crime that occurred in the story a major concern for people today?

Barriers to Appreciating Mysteries

Some readers simply will not enjoy mysteries. Other children, or their parents and teachers, may be concerned that mysteries will serve as "blueprints" for violence, crime, and antisocial-social behavior. Teachers and librarians may also have their own bias against mysteries, believing them not to be "legitimate literature." For readers who want to read mysteries, it is important that these issues be addressed.

Youth Violence and Crime

Youth violence and crime is a concern for everyone. Although overall crime is decreasing according to the FBI, youth violence and crime in the United States is much higher than in other developed nations. Gangs, drug abuse, access to weapons, and social welfare crises create a society where more children are involved in crime than ever before in our history. We cannot discount the increase in violence and homicides attributed to children.

Given these concerns, it is legitimate to ask whether reading mysteries, and especially true crime, could contribute to violence or spur a child to commit a criminal act. While these are legitimate questions, the answer is a resounding "no." Studies have repeatedly shown that young people who commit crimes are those who do not find safe methods to express their feelings and alternative ways to test adolescent bravado. In her book, *Crime*, Marianne LeVert points to conditions that lead to low self-esteem and self-hatred as the causes of juvenile criminal behavior. Violent juveniles lack feelings of empathy, remorse, or guilt. Indeed, Walter Dean Myers, in discussing his research before writing *Monster*, also discusses the feelings of disassociation that most violent offenders express in relation to their actions. About his interviews with incarcerated young people, Myers says, "They would often talk in the active first person about themselves, and then switch to the passive voice when talking about the crime" (701–2). The offenders do not accept responsibility for their actions.

Statistically, most crimes committed by juveniles are committed by a small number of teenagers—that is, the same young person usually commits several crimes. Many scholars and researchers believe that today's criminals do not know right from wrong and are unable to link present actions with future consequences. Use books such as *Crime*, edited by Paul A. Winters, to encourage debate about the causes of crime, how to deal with crime, and methods of prevention. Winters also provides an excellent list of organizations to contact for additional information on crime and crime prevention.

It is also important to help young people recognize that while sensational crimes and horrific violence makes the news, these acts are rare. According to the Bureau of Justice Statistics' *Indicators of School Crime and Safety, 2002*, crime in schools is declining and decreased by half between 1993 and 2000. Still, in 2000, 1.9 million crimes of violence or theft were committed against youth aged 12–18 (vi). Problems like bullying have certainly increased and *Youth Risk Behavior Surveillance—United States, 2001*, a study by Jo Anne Grunbaum with the Centers for Disease Control, reported that 17.4% of high school students stated that they carried a weapon during the 30 days prior to the survey. While not discounting the violence and crime many people face, mysteries generally have a just conclusion and societal values are upheld. Discussing the crimes read about in a mystery novel can help students understand mortality and develop empathy.

Media Violence

Most researchers are convinced that there is a link between the media and the increase in violence in our society, particularly when combined with detrimental family and social conditions. The American Psychiatric Association declared that after three decades of research there is no question that exposure to media violence increases aggressive behavior in children (Psychiatric Effects). Although no studies to date have empirically linked violence in the media to criminal behavior, it is accurate to say that today's children have much more exposure to movies, television programming, and video games that include violent activities.

Child clinical psychologist and crime novelist Jonathan Kellerman has a greater than average interest in whether reading mysteries and crime novels contribute to violence. In *Savage Spawn: Reflections on Violent Children*, Kellerman points out that while numerous studies have "produced correlations and other statistical associations between media violence and aggression in children, not a single causal link between media violence and criminality has ever been produced" (72). He further points out that serial killers who use images "to stimulate associations between sexuality and violence" (77) collect printed violence, particularly violent pornography and graphic, sensationalized true crime magazines. However, the violent tendencies were already present in their personalities! If it were possible to create a world without "bloody books" and free of violent media, these psychopaths would probably still have killed. According to Kellerman, "antisocial behavior in childhood often lays the foundations for a durable pattern of adult criminality" (18).

With the exception of pornographic books, none of the studies on media violence find printed materials or books to be a concern. Responding to questions regarding media violence, Dr. L. Rowell Huesmann stated, "A more difficult question concerns how great literature that includes violence should be portrayed for children, e.g., Macbeth, Hamlet. My own view is that again the benefits from understanding the themes in great literature about human failings and the consequences of them outweighs concerns about effects of violence." While most of the mysteries children will read cannot be compared with Shakespeare's writing, children who are reading, whether they are reading mysteries, science fiction, true crime, or Bible stories, are finding constructive outlets for their energies. They are learning empathy and developing feelings for people from different lifestyles. Readers also have control over the experience. Unlike watching television or movies, the reader can skip passages that evoke an uncomfortable level of fear or stress.

Frequently, children who are readers are also well connected to adults in their lives—librarians, teachers, parents—who recommend books to them, discuss what they have read, and listen to their concerns. Fascination with weapons, cruelty to animals, and frequent fighting are more consistently accurate indicators of violent and homicidal actions than an individual's choice of reading materials. We need not fear that reading mysteries will lead to a life of crime!

Professional Resource: The National School Safety Center offers a checklist for educators that delineates the characteristics of youth who have caused school-associated violence <http://www.nssc1.org/reporter/checklist.htm>.

The Literary Value (or Lack Thereof)

Another barrier to appreciating mystery novels is the erroneous belief by some people, including scholars and academics, that by definition mystery novels are not literature and are therefore not worthy of reading. Teachers are occasionally chastised for spending valuable class time studying a mystery book. To some extent, one might be tempted to ask, "Who cares if mysteries are literature?" Indeed, the same question could be asked of most books written in any genre. One must also reflect on how "literature" is defined and what criteria are being used to determine literary value. Often books that have become classics and have lasting value were ignored or disregarded by critics at the time of publication. Regardless of what critics think about the literary value of her writing, all of Agatha Christie's books are usually in print at any moment, and more of her books have been translated into foreign languages than those of any other author except Shakespeare.

Even within adult publishing, roughly two-thirds of all mysteries published are in series. On a literary scale, most of what is published each year, in any genre, has more entertainment value than lasting literary significance. It is also hard to fight the market—the Babysitter's Club mysteries sold over 100 million copies. No matter how much educators and librarians bemoan their lack of literary value, kids (and adults) who read for pleasure will read what they enjoy, not what they are told to read. At least those who are reading can be introduced to better books.

There are critics who question the value of reading anything but high quality material, and who doubt that children who primarily read genre books will make the transition to better selections. There are also those who question whether there is any value to developing the habit of reading if the reading material is "fluff." Obviously, teachers, librarians, and parents will want to offer children a rich assortment of reading material and select books appropriate to educational goals. At the same time, we should avoid being elitist and acknowledge every person's right to select leisure reading according to their own taste. Many children's mysteries are written by accomplished authors, win literary awards, and stand up to repeated readings and study. Nevertheless, even those that do not become classics offer opportunities for young people to enjoy reading.

Child Safety and Mysteries

It is legitimate to include crime prevention, personal safety, and criminal justice into classroom studies and library programs. Indeed, mysteries can be used as the starting point for a discussion about personal safety and security. What might the character have done differently? How can we be aware of potential danger around us?

The Berenstain Bears and No Guns Allowed by Stan and Jan Berenstain looks at the culture of violence. Some of the factors that the principal at the school in Bear Country identifies as contributors to violence are rudeness, trash talking and name-calling, and acts of "light" violence such as pushing and shoving. The teachers discuss potential solutions, including banning all violent literature from the library. They also look at the influence of cliques, the availability of guns, and violence on television. Teachers and parents can use the book to open discussion with young people.

Professional Resources:
- National PTA resources include posters, a community violence prevention toolkit, and brochures <http://www.pta.org>.
- National Crime Prevention Council resources include McGruff 'Toons Kit and *Stopping School Violence: A Dozen Things Parents, Students, Teachers, Law Enforcement, Principals, and the Rest of Us Can Do*. Many items are available in Spanish <http://www.weprevent.org>.

Chapter 4

Looking at Series Mysteries

"I am afraid that my explanation may disillusion you, but it has always been my habit to hide none of my methods, either from my friend Watson or from anyone who might take an intelligent interest in them." —"The Reigate Puzzle"

Why Series?

What is a series book? Some writers begin a book anticipating that it will be the first in a series, while others find that they enjoy the characters and want to know more about them after the first book is finished. Sometimes the author uses the same characters in more than one book, but does not label the books as a series. While there are exceptions, author and reader generally acknowledge that one protagonist will be at the center of every book in the series. The books take place in, or originate from, the same location, or there is a plausible reason for changing the locale. Series books usually follow a formula: the protagonist is introduced to the reader, important information from past stories is synopsized for those who are joining in the middle of the series, the author moves quickly to the plot, and there is more dialogue than description. Readers get to know the detective (who might not age over the course of the series) and learn more details about his or her life over the course of the series.

Series books of any type for children have always been controversial. Kids love them, try to collect every title available, voraciously consume them, and do not care that they are not great literature. Parents, teachers, and librarians often lament that children will not read anything else and profess not to understand the appeal of reading "the same thing" over and over. Adults sometimes worry that kids who read series are wasting time that could be spent reading better literature and that reading what is often essentially the same story repeatedly will dull the imagination (Saltman). Critics loudly criticize series books because they are not great literature, usually follow a formula, and may not be well written, or they ignore them altogether. Librarians anguish over which series to purchase, how many titles are enough in a series, and whether to spend precious collection development budgets on materials that may be ignored next year.

As reading guru Jim Trelease and other experts have repeatedly pointed out, "What children read is less important than the fact that they read ..." (149). Additionally, Trelease points out that Professor G. Robert Carlson's research, *Voices of Readers*, demonstrated that "a preponderance of the readers began their personal reading with series books like Nancy Drew and the Hardy Boys, often reading as though they were addicted to the subject" (44). When Trelease surveyed 850 teachers about their favorite childhood books, regardless of quality, the Nancy Drew series ranked number four in votes, behind *Little Women, Heidi*, and *Little House in the Big Woods* but in front of *Charlotte's Web!* The Boxcar Children series ranked number six. One-third of the 31 titles ranked were associated with a series (152–153).

Regardless of what adults think about them, many children love to read series books, and especially mystery series. We should not worry about kids who are reading, regardless of what they are reading. Many would agree with Ruth Cline and William McBride that "readers of trash have a chance to improve their literary taste; nonreaders have no taste to improve"(11). Most people who read series eventually move on to better literature. At the same time, let's not be hypocritical—many adults read what could be considered pretty mindless series books (romances, mysteries, westerns, suspense) because these books offer us the same escapism, the same familiar environment, and the same predictability that kids find in series written for them.

While many youngsters do love mystery series, a mystery series will not appeal to every reader. James Howe, author of the Bunnicula series, disliked them; therefore, as a child, he disliked all mysteries (The Horn Book). Indeed, the same elements that attract many young readers to series dissuaded him from reading them. While series are popular, the important thing is that every reader has choices.

Series books reflect the current interests and trends of the time. They often come and go according to what is currently new and interesting and reflect popular culture. Most libraries long ago discarded books in the Choose Your Own Adventure series, making room for Scooby-Doo mysteries. Other series have remained popular for decades and reflect either the higher quality of writing by authors like Donald J. Sobol and David A. Adler or the enduring personality of characters like Sherlock Holmes, Nancy Drew, and the Boxcar Children. In some cases, the publisher has updated the series to maintain freshness or has released companion series that appeal to a younger audience than the originals did. Series popularity may also vary geographically: Hank the Cowdog is a perennial favorite in the West but may not be as popular in New England.

Recent series have entered the realm of computers and the Internet. Series such as Cyber.kdz by Bruce Balan and Danger.com by Jordan Cray use computers and the Internet to tie the books together. *The Vanishing Chip*, the first title in the Misfits, Inc. series by Mark Delany, involves the theft of a valuable computer chip. Some studies have indicated that children who use computers are also readers and they want to combine their interests. Statistical research indicates that children are giving up television rather than reading to gain additional computer time. *Kids & Media @ the New Millennium: a Comprehensive National Analysis of Children's Media Use* found that kids who spend a lot of time with any media tend to use other types as well.

Stratemeyer and the Syndicate

Although he did not invent the series book, Edward Stratemeyer started the movement. According to Carol Billman, it is "no coincidence that the Hardy Boys and all their look-alike Stratemeyer contemporaries throughout the 1920s and 1930s ... belong to the milestone epoch in American detective fiction for adults. The boys' detective books are the timely offspring of work by such writers as S.S. Van Dine, the creators of Ellery Queen, Dashell Hammett, Erle Stanley Gardner, and then Raymond Chandler ... soft-boiled though they may be in comparison" (Billman. Stratemeyer Syndicate, 11–12). Billman provides similar links between Nancy Drew and the popular writings of other authors at that time like Mary Roberts Rinehart, whose book, *The Circular Staircase,* according to Billman, served as a model for the girl detective (12).

Stratemeyer participated in the production of more than 900 books for children and reshaped series novels, moving them out of the seedy realm of dime novels into the sphere of more legitimate publishing. It often comes as a surprise that teams of writers, rather than a single author, wrote these popular books. There has been an ever-changing stream of writers, many just beginning their careers, for the books in the Stratemeyer series.

Although Stratemeyer began his writing career in the late 1890s, the first Hardy Boys book was not published until 1927. Nancy Drew followed three years later and was the last series the syndicate introduced. As Deidre Johnson concludes in her study, the surprise with Edward Stratemeyer is that it took him more than 60 years to develop what became the penultimate mystery series for children! Many of his books have transcended American culture and have been translated into other languages.

Leslie McFarlane, the first ghostwriter for the Hardy Boys series, had written titles in another Stratemeyer series but says in his autobiography that he strived to achieve a higher quality of writing with the new series and added humor and other touches to reach out to boys. The first book, *The Tower Treasure*, retains its popularity to this day due in large measure to the combination of adventure and mystery. The series have been revised to update technology and styles, and to remove racial and ethnic stereotyping. Some books were streamlined to be shorter and more accessible to younger readers or were re-written entirely to replace outdated plots. In 1987, Simon and Schuster, which purchased the Stratemeyer Syndicate, began issuing new series, including "The Hardy Boys Casefiles" and "Frank and Joe Hardy: The Clues Brothers," to attract readers at different age levels.

Nancy Drew first appeared in *The Secret of the Old Clock* published in 1930. Mildred Wirt Benson wrote many of the original books and Stratemeyer's daughter, Harriet Adams, ghostwrote others. While Nancy is as adventurous as the Hardy Boys, much of her sleuthing takes place indoors and the plots are more genteel and cerebral. Nancy refuses to take money for solving her cases, although she frequently does accept a souvenir or memento. Nancy's self-reliance and autonomy set her up as a role model for today's "girl power." Her skill, training, and abilities counter stereotypes of female abilities, yet Nancy remains feminine. Spin-off series include "Nancy Drew on Campus," "The Nancy Drew Files," and "Nancy Drew Notebooks."

Web Resources:

- The Stratemeyer site includes links to pages for Nancy Drew and the Hardy Boys, as well as other Syndicate series <http://www.stratemeyer.org>.
- The Nancy Drew site lists every book in the original and spin-off series and offers articles that explain Nancy's popularity <http://www.nancydrew.com>.

Early dime novels were often sensational and trashy, deemed unworthy of being read in "polite" society. Stratemeyer made series books acceptable for young readers; however, librarians have always bemoaned the fact that children often read series books instead of "good" literature. In 1929, the *Wilson Bulletin* encouraged librarians to weed books in series from their collections. Many of the very points that attract criticism are the aspects that make these books so popular: predictability, simplistic characters, and fast-paced action.

By the 1960s, attitudes changed and librarians now generally welcome almost any book that encourages children to read. More importantly, as Billman points out in her article, "The Child Reader as Sleuth," series books can set the stage for children to read and appreciate more demanding literature precisely because they have reinforced for the young reader the very structure of the novel in general, and of mysteries in particular. Even the most predictable series mystery provides the contrasts between known and unknown, which Billman indicates are important to learning to be a successful reader.

A Look at Major Series

One of the great opportunities in children's literature derives from the fact that teachers and librarians receive a fresh audience every year. Because of this, good books remain in print for decades. For young people who are ready to move beyond the series, additional reading suggestions are listed.

Encyclopedia Brown

Encyclopedia Brown, Boy Detective by Donald Sobol was published in 1963. Because the stories are short, they are popular as transitional books for new readers, moving the reader from basal readers into "chapter" books. Each short story includes all of the clues, albeit sometimes very subtle clues, that the reader needs in order to match wits with the boy detective.

Leroy "Encyclopedia" Brown is the 10-year-old son of the Idaville police chief. Blessed with a photographic memory, he recalls everything he reads. He also has the ability to observe a situation and notice what is missing or hidden. Whenever his father has a tough case, he describes it to Encyclopedia who discerns the important information and deduces the solution. During school vacations, Encyclopedia runs his own detective agency. Before disclosing the solution, Sobol always asks a question and allows the reader to suggest the solution.

In *Encyclopedia Brown and the Case of the Treasure Hunt*, Sobol introduced Sally Kimball, a junior partner in Encyclopedia's detective agency. For almost four decades, Encyclopedia has remained the same age. The stories are great for reading aloud in the classroom and for library use because they encourage readers (or listeners) to pay close attention to every detail.

Art Activity: Encyclopedia hangs out a sign advertising his detective agency. Provide pieces of tagboard and markers or other art supplies. Let students design a sign for their own detective agency. Discuss some of the decisions that must be made before the sign can be designed—what the agency will be called, how much the detectives will charge, what the logo will look like, and so on.

Math Activity: Encyclopedia charges 25¢ a day plus expenses. Is this a reasonable rate? What expenses might a detective have that would be charged to the client? Research what is needed to run a business and determine the costs for office space, a phone, and supplies. Ask the students to calculate how many cases they would need to take at the rate they charge in order to stay in business.

Suggested Books:
The Case of the Wiggling Wig: a McGurk Mystery by E.W. Hildick.
The Great Brain by John D. Fitzgerald.
How Can a Brilliant Detective Shine in the Dark? by Linda Bailey.
The Mysterious Lights and Other Cases by Seymour Simon.
Solve-It-Yourself Mysteries: Detective Club Puzzlers by Hy Conrad.

Nate the Great

Marjorie Weinman Sharmat began her writing career at the age of eight by publishing neighborhood happenings in her own newspaper. Her desire to be a detective merged with her writing talent with the 1972 publication of *Nate the Great*.

Nate is a nine-year-old boy who wears a Sherlock Holmes deerstalker hat and trench coat and carries a magnifying glass. Although Sharmat writes with controlled vocabulary, the stories have a "just the facts" tone that is perfect for new readers practicing their skills. Even though they are written for beginning readers, the cases can be complex and Nate methodically follows the clues. His companion, a dog named Sludge, accompanies him on his cases and Nate always finds time to eat his favorite food, pancakes.

Guest Speaker: Read *Nate the Great and Me: The Case of the Fleeing Fang*. Fang runs away and Nate's friends do some investigating to find the missing dog. Invite someone from the local humane society or animal shelter to talk about what to do if a pet gets lost. It takes some real detective work to find a lost animal!

Science Activity: Nate often writes secret messages. Use lemon juice to write a secret message. Dip a stylus (any blunt stick, a rounded toothpick, or the blunt end of a cotton swab) in the juice and write on white paper. To further hide your secret message, write something in regular ink or pencil on the paper. In order to read your secret writing, the recipient will need to hold the piece of paper close to a light bulb. Move the paper around but do not let it touch the bulb. The heat from the bulb will turn the lemon juice brown and the secret message will appear.

> **Suggested Books:**
> *The Case of the Hungry Stranger* by Crosby Newell Bonsall.
> *Detective Donut and the Wild Goose Chase* by Bruce Whatley
>   and Rosie Smith.
> *The Mystery of the Missing Dog* by Elizabeth Levy.
> *Mystery on the Docks* by Thatcher Hurd.
> *Robbery at the Diamond Dog Diner* by Eileen Christelow.

Cam Jansen

This series by David A. Adler features a girl detective, Cam Jansen. Her real name is Jennifer, but her nickname is short for "The Camera," which describes her photographic memory. Whenever she wants to remember something important, she blinks her eyes and says, "Click" as her mental camera takes a photograph. Cam is based loosely on a boy Adler knew in elementary school and many of the stories are based on things that have happened to Adler and his family.

The first book in the series, *Cam Jansen and the Mystery of the Stolen Diamonds,* was published in 1980. The series is geared toward readers who are moving from controlled vocabulary readers to chapter books. Each book ends with a "memory quiz" inviting the reader to look at a picture and answer questions to see how much he or she can remember. In 1996, the first book in a related easy-to-read series, *Young Cam Jansen and the Missing Cookie,* was published featuring Cam as an eight-year-old.

Science Activity: Talk about how a camera works and then make a pinhole camera. Books like *Click! A Book About Cameras and Taking Pictures* by Gail Gibbons or *The Camera* by Joseph Wallace can help explain the principles of photography. Kodak offers simple instructions for making a pinhole camera on its Web site at <http://www.kodak.com/global/en/consumer/education/lessonPlans/pinholeCamera/>.

> **Suggested Books:**
> *Aunt Eater Loves a Mystery* by Doug Cushman.
> *Basil of Baker Street* by Eve Titus.
> *The Case of the Elevator Duck* by Polly B. Berends.
> *The Creepy Computer Mystery* by Elizabeth Levy.
> *Flatfoot Fox and the Case of the Missing Schoolhouse* by Clifford Eth.

A to Z Mysteries

Like adult author Sue Grafton, Ron Roy is working his way through the alphabet in the titles of his books. From *The Absent Author* (published in 1997) to *The Talking T-Rex* (published in 2003), readers will want to read to Z. Dink, Josh, and Ruth Rose find treasure off the coast of Florida, discover who stole a precious emerald from a New York museum, and catch the culprit who injured a rare bird. Although the books are predictable, they are fun for young detectives.

Writing Activity: In *The Absent Author*, Dink writes to his favorite author, inviting him to visit the class. Surprised that the invitation was accepted, Dink suspects foul play when Wallis Wallace does not show up. Ask the students to write a letter to their favorite author telling him or her why they enjoy reading the author's book. Although the letters do not actually have to be mailed (in fact, many authors include an e-mail address on their Web sites as an alternative means of communication), they can be sent to the author through the publisher of the most recent book. Keep in mind that it can take time for letters to reach the author, and many authors are busy and will not respond immediately. Also, be cautious about having students invite an author to visit their classroom; this is a wonderful activity but will usually have a cost associated with it and schedules can book up two years in advance.

> **Suggested Books:**
> *The Case of the Ghostwriter* by James Preller.
> *The Ghost of Fossil Glen* by Cynthia DeFelice.
> *The House Of Dies Drear* by Virginia Hamilton.
> *Janie's Private Eyes* by Zilpha Keatley Snyder.
> *The Mysterious Matter of I. M. Fine* by Diane Stanley.

Hank the Cowdog

John Erickson hit the trail running in 1983 with his first mystery, *The Original Adventures of Hank the Cowdog*. As Head of Ranch Security, Hank discovers that there has been a murder on the ranch, only to find himself accused of the crime. Told in the first person, the crime-solving dog is an easy-going guy, full of wit and cowboy wisdom. He understands that there is a thin line between heroism and stupidity but still finds himself in some hair-raising adventures. Hank and his sidekick Drover are based on dogs Erickson knew when he worked a ranch.

Craft Activity: Make a bolo tie with Western shapes. Use a die-cut machine to create Western shapes like a howling coyote, a boot, a cactus, or longhorns. Cover with aluminum foil (or silver or gold foil) to give the shape a metallic look. Use a round toothpick or craft stick to smooth the corners and give a nice fit. Glue a short piece of plastic straw horizontally on the back of the shape. String bolo or other cord through the straw allowing the ends to hang down below the shape. Tie a knot on each end to keep the cord from going back through the straw.

Glue jewels or stones to the bolo, if desired. Craft stores sell bolo cord (and, if you want to get fancy, bola slides and tips).

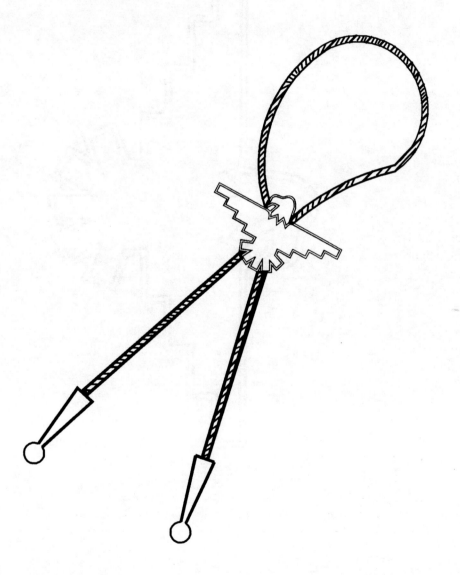

Figure 4.1: Bolo Tie Illustration

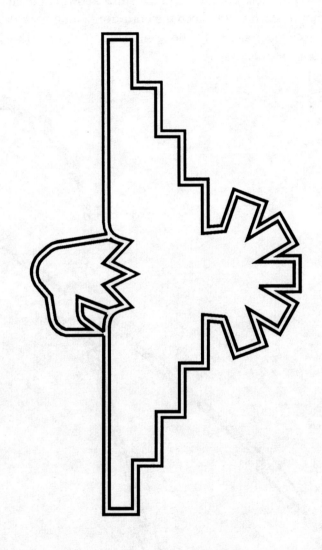

Figure 4.2: Bolo Tie Pattern

Writing Activity: Write a letter to Hank. What do you want to know about ranch life? Students should then exchange letters and research the answers to the questions about ranch life.

Geography Activity: Find Perryton on a map of Texas. Figure out how far it is from where you live to Hank's ranch. Can you find the fastest route to Hank? Use the Internet to find interesting information about Perryton. (What is the town's nickname? Why is April 14, 1935, called "Black Sunday?")

Web Resource: Visit Hank's official Web site to learn about the ranch and all of the characters, enter contests, and play games <http://www.hankthecowdog.com/>.

Suggested Books:
Bunnicula: A Rabbit Tale of Mystery by James Howe.
Freddy the Detective by Walter Brooks.
The Mysterious Disappearance of Leon (I Mean Noel) by Ellen Raskin.
The Mystery of King Karfu by Doug Cushman.
Wanted ... Mud Blossom by Betsy Byars.

Lemony Snicket

The Bad Beginning: Book the First was published in 1999 on the heels of the Harry Potter phenomenon and struck the fancy of many of Harry's fans. Told in a mock-Gothic, melodramatic style, the humorous series chronicles the unfortunate events in the lives of three orphaned children. The author is a mysterious person, about whom, readers are told, little is known. Daniel Handler usually shows up in place of Lemony Snicket to talk about the books at conferences and in presentations and always has a convoluted story to explain why Snicket could not be there. Each book warns the reader that there are no happy endings in these stories but, in spite of their tone, the books are morality tales that offer readers humor and mystery.

Violet, Klaus, and Sunny Baudelaire were orphaned when their parents died in a fire. They have been left a fortune that Violet cannot claim until she is an adult. Until that time, according to the will, the children must live with a blood relative, each of whom turns out to be incompetent or cruel or dies by the end of the story. They must also try to avoid the dastardly intentions of evil Count Olaf, who claims to be their uncle and wants to steal their fortune. Violet is an inventor and Klaus is a skilled researcher. Along with baby Sunny, the kids try to thwart Count Olaf's villainous efforts and figure out how they can live a safe and peaceful life. Nickelodeon plans to release a movie based on the Snicket books late in 2004.

Class Discussion: Many of the characters in the Snicket books take their names from other literary or historical characters—Baudelaires, Poe, Nero, Gengis. Talk about the names you would use for new characters. Pick a name and describe what that character would look like and how he or she would behave in your Lemony Snicket book.

Vocabulary Builder: Lemony Snicket includes a wonderful assortment of vocabulary words, intriguing phrases, and anagrams in his books. Ask each student to find a couple of interesting words or phrases and list them on index cards. Students can then find definitions of words and write sentences using the words. Phrases can be looked up in *Brewer's Dictionary of Phrase & Fable.* Then students can share the origins of words in small group discussions.

Art Activity: Create wanted posters to aid in the capture of Count Olaf. Remember that he is an actor and likes disguises, so be sure to show some of them and provide a written description of what he looks like. You might want to include information about the crimes for which Count Olaf has been accused—murder, robbery, fraud, bribery, and poor hygiene.

Class Project: Lemony Snicket: The Unauthorized Autobiography uses photographs, diary entries, letters, newspaper clippings, screenplays, and other documents to tell the life story of Mr. Snicket. As a group, select another author or detective and write that person's unauthorized autobiography in the same manner. Use the Internet, newspaper and periodical indices, publisher's Web sites, book jackets, and other resources to collect information. When all else fails, create your own documents!

Web Resource: The Lemony Snicket Web site warns visitors to go to any other site, but if they persist, the site offers information about books to read instead of these, activities, and questions for discussion related to the books <http://www.lemonysnicket.com>.

Suggested Books:
Artemis Fowl by Eoin Colfer.
The House With A Clock In Its Walls by John Bellairs.
Pure Dead Magic by Debi Gliori.
The Ruby in the Smoke by Philip Pullman.
Wolves of Willoughby Chase by Joan Aiken.

Chet Gecko

With his tongue planted firmly in cheek, Bruce Hale began to chronicle the stories of a great detective, who just happens to be a lizard. With plenty of puns, double entendres, and allusions to Raymond Chandler, Dashiell Hammett, and Lew Archer, Hale parodies the hard-boiled style of writing. Chet Gecko is a fourth grader who attends Emerson Hickey Elementary School. He is a wisecracking lizard who talks in the style of 1940s films. Like Philip Marlowe or Sam Spade, Chet is a hero with many flaws, a knight-errant, a lizard with attitude. His sidekick is Natalie Attired, a "spiffy mockingbird with a detective sense sharp enough to cut cheese."

Language Arts Activity: Bruce Hale includes many puns in his mysteries. Talk about puns and why they are funny, and then make up some puns of your own. Puns can be the use of words that sound like other words (e.g., alarms = what an octopus is (all arms)) or the witty transposition of words (e.g., kleptomaniac: One who can't help himself from helping himself.). Spoonerisms and Tom Swifties ("I know who turned off the lights," Tom hinted darkly.) are also considered puns. Hold a pun contest, jest for the pun of it!

Writing Activity: Each Chet Gecko mystery begins with an interesting lead-in paragraph that sets the tone for the story. For example, *The Chameleon Wore Chartreuse* begins "It was a hot day in September. The kind of day when kindergartners wake up cranky from their naps." Discuss why this line attracts the reader. Let students try their hand at writing a couple of sentences to begin a mystery.

Chinatown Mysteries

Although there are currently only three books, this series by Laurence Yep is important because of his reputation as an outstanding writer and the dearth of other mysteries for children that feature Asian characters. The series is set in San Francisco's Chinatown and features 12-year-old Lily Lew and her great aunt. Aunt Tiger Lil is a former Chinese-American movie star, now working as a public relations guru and erstwhile detective. The first book, *The Case of the Goblin Pearls*, was published in 1997. These action-packed mysteries introduce Chinese and Chinese-American culture and Yep includes some great red herrings.

Craft Activity: Make a Chinese lantern with a piece of construction paper (12" x 18"), scissors, and markers, crayons, or colored pencils. First, decorate the paper with Chinese symbols. Then, fold the paper lengthwise and cut from the fold every one to one-and-a-half inches, stopping about two inches from the open ends. After the student is finished cutting, open the paper and bend it into a circle shape. Staple or glue the edges together. Add a strip of paper or yarn to the top to act as a handle.

Figure 4.3: Chinese Lantern Illustration

Other Series, Briefly

Sammy Keyes

Sammy Keyes And The Hotel Thief, the first title in Wendelin Van Draanen's series, was published in 1998. Seventh-grader Sammy has many problems, most stemming from her brash, tomboy attitude, but some originating in her unconventional lifestyle. While her mother is off in Hollywood finding herself, Sammy lives with her grandmother. She is comfortable with her life in a senior citizen's complex and Sammy has found her calling as a crime solver and gets into crazy capers. The plots blend mystery, humor, and coming-of-age angst with situations that, while far-fetched, are not out of the question for a contemporary girl. Sammy is smart, brave, and resourceful and will appeal to many readers who are ready to move beyond formula series.

Mysteries in Our National Parks

Beginning with *Wolf Stalker*, the mother-daughter team of Gloria Skurzynski and Alane Ferguson use America's national parks as the backdrop for this fast-paced series. As a wildlife biologist, mother Olivia Landon gets temporary assignments that require her to move from location to location. This allows her children, Jack and Ashley, to find adventures they would never find closer to home. In addition to the geography of each locale, the mysteries involve ecology, endangered wildlife, or environmental issues. The details are well researched and exact and a park map helps readers understand the setting, providing a solid connection for family vacation reading. While never preachy, the stories demonstrate good family values. As of early 2003, there were 12 titles in the series, but the series may eventually cover all the national parks in the country.

P.C. Hawke Mysteries

Paul Zindel wrote this series about a high-school student, Philip Christopher (P.C.) Hawke, and his best friend, Mackenzie Riggs. Mac's mother is the New York City coroner, so it is through her that the kids get involved in cases. Each book begins with a page from "the terrifying files of P.C. Hawke" that sets up the story. Beginning with *Scream Museum*, the friends travel to exotic locations, including the Amazon River, Venice Beach, and the Bronx Zoo, to solve cases. The pair goes to a private school where half of the kids are SRF (spawn of the rich and famous). Mac wears Doc Martens, and she uses snappy dialogue. P.C. and Mac seem to have absolute freedom to leave school whenever they are needed for a case. Solving the cases involves more physical activity and brainpower than technology. Despite the fact that P.C. and Mac are in high school, and that the cases involve murders, the reading level is at about fifth grade and the format of the books will appeal to middle-school readers. With minimal violence and fast-paced adventure, the books are suitable for the audience and may encourage them to read other books by Zindel.

The High-Rise Private Eyes

Cynthia Rylant and illustrator G. Brian Karas team up for an easy-to-read mystery series that features the case-cracking skills of Bunny Brown and Jack Jones, a raccoon. The duo banters and bickers and has a lot of fun. Beginning with *The Case of the Missing Monkey*, each book has four chapters, and Karas's illustrations help new reader's focus in on the facts. The cases are simple and the friends have fun finding the culprit.

Christian Series

It is often difficult for parochial schools and public libraries to find series books that satisfy the requests of Christian families. For mysteries, several series are available that are as well written as mainstream series and should be considered for their popularity. (Although there are some single title mysteries that feature children from non-Christian religions, series mysteries are currently limited to Christianity.)

X-Country Adventures

Each book in the X-County Adventures series by Bob Schaller features two siblings and focuses on their adventures in a specific state. Ashley and Adam respect their parents and get along with each other. Each book includes a "Fun Facts File" with information about the geography, economy, history, and culture of the locales included in the mystery. Maps help readers follow the Arlington's route and Schaller provides suggested Web sites and other readings for those who want to know more about the state visited, the activities involved, or the other subjects in each book. Eventually Schaller expects to have written about all 50 states, so if your favorite has not been covered, it will be!

Jennie McGrady

Jennie McGrady is a young sleuth from the Nancy Drew mold. The first book, *Too Many Secrets*, was published in 1993. Jennie loves to read and her mother is a freelance magazine writer, allowing Jennie to travel around the world solving mysteries. Patricia H. Rushford's stories feature stalking, hate crimes, swindling, bombings, and other crimes out of today's headlines, but Jennie often whispers a prayer as she faces danger. *Silent Witness* was nomination for an Edgar Award for Best Young Adult Mystery.

The Cooper Kids Adventure Series

Lila and Jay frequently join their father, a Biblical archeologist, in remote and exotic locales where they inevitably become embroiled in a mystery and face danger. Reminiscent of Indiana Jones, the series by Frank Peretti is aimed at middle-school readers. The first book, published in 1990, is *The Door in the Dragon's Throat*.

The Veritas Project

This series for teenagers by Frank Peretti begins with *Hangman's Curse* published in 2001. Nate and Sarah, and twin's Elijah and Elisha, are part of the Veritas Project team. They travel around the country working with the FBI and other organizations to solve crimes and find the truth behind mysterious events.

Evaluating Series and Moving Readers Beyond

In some cases, we should evaluate series books using the same criteria we use for other books. Books that will remain in our collections for many years or books by established and highly regarded authors need to be selected based on the same rigorous standards we use to make other selections. However, with many mystery series, libraries will purchase what is popular, regardless of the quality of the writing, to meet demand.

Children have the same right as adults to find what they want in a public library. Each library must determine how much of the limited collection budget can be spent on items of ephemeral interest, so while we may not buy every book in the Scooby-Doo mystery series, we probably should have some. School libraries, with even more limitations on resources, may need to rely on donations, free books received from book fairs, or funds from the PTA to buy books that will have short-term popularity. A major part of building a good relationship with children includes showing respect for their interests and demonstrating that we have some understanding of popular culture and trends. It is also important for schools, in fostering literacy, to purchase books that children read for pleasure. We do not want to turn away one of our largest ready-made audiences—the kids who read series books—because we do not have what they want to read.

As the examples demonstrate, series books can be good literature and provide a quality reading experience. As has been previously noted, many reading experts believe that a good teacher or librarian can move a child who reads anything on to reading better material. Ask most adults who are avid readers and they will tell you that they read series books and other simplistic or "mindless" material. In fact, they probably still do! One of the most important things we can do as teachers and librarians is to encourage reading. By allowing children to read what they enjoy, we help them develop a lifelong habit of reading for pleasure, and, if someone reads for pleasure, he or she will almost certainly read for information and personal growth.

Kylene Beers differentiates between avid readers and reluctant readers. Beers notes that reluctant readers want to select books from a very narrow range of choices. Because readers know what to expect from a series, these mysteries help reluctant readers become avid readers. However, reluctant readers also like to have the teacher or librarian read aloud an entire book, giving us the opportunity to introduce reluctant readers to more sophisticated books. While more experienced and expert readers do not necessarily need to hear books read aloud, many will still enjoy the classroom experience. Incorporate books with better quality writing into your classroom reading and library story times. Audiobooks also provide an excellent way to introduce students to books they might not otherwise select.

Public libraries can also use methods to encourage reading that is more challenging. Read aloud to school-aged children. Hold book discussion groups or lunchtime reading events. Encourage reluctant readers to read advance reader copies received from publishers and write reviews that can be published on the library Web site or printed out for others to enjoy. Even viewing the film version of a book can entice readers to try something that might be a little more difficult reading or a bit more sophisticated than would usually appeal to them. Display books face out so that student's are enticed to pick one up. Create clever and attractive bulletin boards that advertise great titles (or better yet, have students create displays and bulletin boards that tell their peers what is good reading).

We all know kids who, when they want to, can and do read difficult material on a subject for which they have a great deal of enthusiasm. Many children are enthusiastic about reading mysteries, so we can tap into that enthusiasm to suggest higher quality reading. It is our job to ensure that when children are ready for better books, they are available. By building a relationship with the readers, by respecting their right to read whatever appeals to them, and by subtly offering alternatives, kids will be more likely to take our suggestions when they are ready to move on to other reading.

Suggested Read-Alouds:
The Case of the Baker Street Irregular by Robert Newman.
Casebook of a Private (Cat's) Eye by Mary Stoltz.
The Egypt Game by Zilpha Keatley Snyder.
The Mark Twain Murders by Laurence Yep.
The Playmaker by J.B. Cheaney.

Suggested Audiobooks:
Alice Rose and Sam by Kathryn Lasky. Recorded Books, 2000.
Ghost Canoe by Will Hobbs. Listening Library, 1999.
Holes by Louis Sachar. Listening Library, 1999.
Sammy Keyes And The Curse Of Moustache Mary
    by Wendelin Van Draanen. Live Oak Media, 2002.

Chapter 5

Suggestions for Integrating Mysteries into the Curriculum

"Education never ends, Watson. It is a series of lessons with the greatest for the last." — "The Adventure of the Red Circle"

One of the best ways to help children enjoy literature is by including trade books in the school curriculum and making reading a part of classroom activities. Mysteries fit into many areas of the curriculum, making it easy to introduce concepts in a manner that makes them interesting and enjoyable. Mysteries can be fiction or nonfiction, and, because so many children enjoy them, they are often willing to try something new.

Mysteries have a great deal of potential for encouraging reluctant readers to read and challenging gifted students to expand their learning. They offer opportunities for students to achieve the higher-level thinking skills presented in Bloom's Taxonomy as they gain knowledge about the events surrounding the mystery, explain what has happened, interpret events, analyze and categorize clues, collect facts to form a hypothesis, and assess their skill at solving the mystery.

Bloom's Taxonomy

- Knowledge
- Comprehension
- Application
- Analysis
- Synthesis
- Evaluation

Feel free to tailor these suggestions to your classroom needs. Grade levels are not indicated for the curriculum ideas because abilities and interests vary widely. Substitute another book, or adapt the activities to a book you want to use or have available. Modify the books and learning experiences to suit the grade level and abilities of your class. The ideas range from very simple, perhaps even obvious, suggestions that you may not have thought of in a while to more complex and elaborate ideas that will require more time or resources. Adapt them to your needs, students' abilities, and your resources.

URLs for Web sites were accurate at the time of printing. Be sure to verify that they are still active before using them in class or the library media center. Never provide URLs to students unless you have verified that the information is still active and the site is still appropriate!

Science

Book to Integrate: Endangered Species

Over the Edge by Gloria Skurzynski and Alane Ferguson.
California Condors are being poisoned in the Grand Canyon. Wildlife biologist Olivia Landon and her kids search for the source of the poison. When Olivia receives a death threat via e-mail, the kids face personal danger from an unexpected source.

Science Discussion: Discuss what it means for a species of animal to be endangered. Distribute lists of endangered species and ask each student to research an animal. Visit the U.S. Fish and Wildlife Services Web site at <http://endangered.fws.gov/> for lists of endangered animals, detailed information on each species, statistics, and related activities.

Fact Finding: List the facts about the Condor that students learn from the book. Use reference sources to find additional information about the bird.

Web Resource: Kids Planet provides a map with information about endangered species at <http://www.kidsplanet.org/factsheets/map.html>.

Ethics: In order to save the species from extinction, the last condor, called AC-9 (short for Adult Condor 9), was captured by the Los Angeles Zoo in 1987. The decision to capture AC-9 was very controversial. Go to <http://www.lazoo.org> for details and a time line. Ask students to find articles from that time and discuss why people protested. List the reasons for capturing the condor; list the reasons for not interfering. Discuss whether the zoo did the right thing by capturing AC-9 in order to save the species. In 2000, the Zoo released a female California Condor back into the wild. What is the total California Condor population today?

Compare and Contrast: Condors are raptors, or birds of prey. List other species of raptors. Students can explore the traits that distinguish raptors from other birds. List the characteristics of all birds and then list how raptors differ. Which species live in your area? Many communities have raptor assistance programs or people who rehabilitate injured birds. Ask a speaker to visit your class; often the speaker will bring a bird that cannot be released.

> *Books to Share:*
> *The Case of the Missing Cutthroats* by Jean Craighead George.
> *The Falcon's Feathers* by Ron Roy.
> *The Kingfisher's Tale* by Mark Delaney.
> *The Panther Mystery* by Gertrude Chandler Warner.

Book to Integrate: Forensic Science

The Wildlife Detectives: How Forensic Scientists Fight Crimes Against Nature
    by Donna M. Jackson.
Using details of an actual case, Jackson explains how scientists examine clues and follow tips to solve crimes against wild animals. Criminals who poach elephant ivory, catch endangered turtles

for soup, and commit other crimes in the name of vanity, greed, or superstition are brought to justice through scientific investigation.

Research: Discuss the ways that wildlife investigators use science to fight crimes that are committed against endangered animals. Although most of these criminals currently get away with their crimes, scientific detectives are making it possible for law enforcement agencies to successfully prosecute those who commit crimes against wildlife. Students could research some of these methods. How are they similar to investigating crimes against people? Is there any value in continuing to fight what might appear to be a losing battle?

Economics: Discuss what can be done to help reduce or eliminate these wildlife crimes. For example, poachers kill wild animals because there are people who will buy products made from the animal. How can we shop wisely to avoid furthering this trade? Students could raise funds to help organizations that work to save endangered species. Research which countries allow the exportation of products made from endangered species. Write letters to the heads of those nations asking that they outlaw this practice.

Geography: As of 2003, 145 countries are committed to the Convention on International Trade in Endangered Species (CITES) of Wild Fauna and Flora, a treaty in effect since 1975. Research CITES. Use a map of the world to pinpoint the countries that have *not* entered into this agreement to protect plants and animals from unregulated international trade (the list is available online at <http://international.fws.gov/cites/citnolop.html>).

> ***Books to Share:***
> *Hoot* by Carl Hiaasen.
> *Shadows in the Water* by Kathyn Lasky.
> *The Case of the Mummified Pigs and Other Mysteries of Nature*
>   by Susan E. Quinlan.

Book to Integrate: Ecology

Who Really Killed Cock Robin? by Jean Craighead George.
When the town mascot dies, foul play is suspected. Tony, an eighth grader who is an expert on robins, is called in to investigate. As he weaves his way through the clues, he realizes that his town is in big trouble.

Science Discussion: Talk about pollution in your town. Jean Craighead George wrote this book in 1971. Discuss whether the pollution problem has improved or become worse since then. Use chart paper to list improvements in one column and work that still needs to be done in another. Tony keeps a notebook because "good notes are the basis of scientific research." List other tools for good research. How many robins live in your neighborhood? Ask organizations like the Sierra Club to talk about your community.

Guest Speaker: Ask an ornithologist, a biologist, or a bird watcher to discuss the effects of pollution on birds and to explain ways that students can help increase the bird population or protect birds from pollution.

Writing Activity: The mayor reported much of what happens to Cock Robin and Mrs. Robin over the local radio station and in the local newspaper. Read the paragraph on page 10, where the mayor describes Mrs. Robin's activities. Ask students to observe a bird or an animal and report it as a radio report or in writing as a sample newspaper article. The local newspaper is called the *Patent Reader*. Decide on a good name for your class newspaper and print some of the sample articles to share with other classes.

Civics Activity: DDT, PCBs, and phosphates are the chemicals suspected of causing Cock Robin's death. In 1977, Congress banned production of DDT and PCBs. However, many pollutants are still permitted. Students could research chemical pollution and write a letter to a local or national politician asking what is being done to reduce pollution.

Web Resource: The Sierra Club Web site at <http://www.sierraclub.org> has background information on issues that effect the environment.

> ***Books to Share:***
> *The Case of the Grand Canyon Eagle* by Dina Anastasio.
> *Deadly Waters* by Gloria Skurzynski and Alane Ferguson.
> *The Fire Bug Connection* by Jean Craighead George.
> *Lostman's River* by Cynthia DeFelice.

Book to Integrate: Botany

Dot and Jabber and the Great Acorn Mystery by Ellen Stoll Walsh.
Two mice investigate the mysteries of nature as they try to figure out why an oak tree has started to grow in an area where there are no other oak trees. Paper collage illustrations highlight the careful investigation and the facts that Dot and Jabber discover.

Arboriculture Activity: Discuss the kinds of trees that grow in your area. Allow students to examine an acorn. Talk about seeds and how they grow into a plant. Plant a tree at your school and have the students take turns watering it.

Physics: Dot and Jabber talk about maple seeds and how they fly around, but acorns are too heavy to fly. Look at different seeds and show examples of some that are heavy and some that are light enough to be distributed by the wind. How are seeds dispersed? What animals help distribute seeds?

Art: Create an oak leaf mobile. Use the pattern provided to reproduce an oak leaf and two acorns and caps for each child. Have children color the leaf and acorns and cut them out. Color the acorn cap and glue it to the top of the acorn. Punch holes where indicated. Use yarn or string to tie the acorns to the leaf. Add yarn to the stem of the oak leaf and hang the mobiles.

> ***Books to Share:***
> *The Case of the Two Masked Robbers* by Lillian Hoban.
> *Dot and Jabber and the Mystery of the Missing Stream* by Ellen Stoll Walsh.
> *Max and Molly and the Mystery of the Missing Honey* by Jung Obrist.
> *The Missing Mitten Mystery* by Steven Kellogg.
> *Who Took the Farmer's Hat?* by Joan Nodset.

Figure 5.1: Oak Leaf Mobile Pattern

Figure 5.2a: Basil Paper Bag Puppet Pattern

Book to Integrate: Small Mammals

Figure 5.2b: Basil Paper Bag Puppet Illustration

Basil of Baker Street by Eve Titus.
The greatest mouse detective in the world acquired his skills literally at the feet of Sherlock Holmes. With his side-kick, Dr. Dawson, Basil solves the kidnapping of two mouse twins. This is one of the most well known pastiches; there are four other titles, some out of print, in the series.

Art: Use the Basil Paper Bag Puppet pattern to create hand puppets. After coloring the pattern, students should cut around the lines and glue the pieces to a paper lunch bag.

Film Resource: View *The Great Mouse Detective*, Disney's version of *Basil of Baker Street*. Discuss how the movie differs from the book.

Analysis and Discussion: This story is considered a pastiche of the original Sherlock Holmes stories. Read a few paragraphs from one of the Sherlock Holmes stories and then compare the words, writing style, and descriptions with this pastiche. What is the difference between plagiarism or copying and writing a pastiche? Select another short mystery story or book. List the elements that make the story unique and interesting. As a class, begin to write your own pastiche.

Scientific Classification: Mice are classified as mammals in the order rodentia (rodents). List other mammals and rodents. Research some of the characteristics of mice. For example, many mice are nocturnal. They also tend to be shy. How would these traits help or hinder a mouse detective's work? Find other mysteries that feature mammals as detectives.

> ***Books to Share:***
> *Basil in the Wild West* by Eve Titus.
> *The Mailbox Mice Mystery* by Juli Mahr.
> *Mystery on the Docks Hurd* by Thatcher Hurd.
> *Picnic with Piggins* by Jane Yolen.
> *The Three Blind Mice Mystery* by Stephen Krensky.

Social Studies

Book to Integrate: Public Safety

Aero and Officer Mike: Police Partners by Joan Plummer Russell.
Aero and Officer Mike have been called the real-life Officer Buckle and Gloria. The police officer and his canine partner work together to keep neighborhoods safe, patrol the streets, and sniff out drugs. Photographs provide details of daily activities.

Research: Bloodhounds, German Shepherds, Bouvier de Flanders, Dobermans, and other breeds of dogs can be trained to help fight crime. While most people think of big, tough dogs like German Shepherds when they think of police dogs, Beagles make great drug-sniffing dogs and Golden Retrievers are often used for search and rescue to find children who have wandered off. Research the various breeds (AKC breed books have good pictures and descriptions) and list the characteristics that might make the breed appropriate for investigative and law enforcement work. List other ways animals help keep us safe.

Psychology: Sirius, an explosive detection dog, was a casualty in the terrorist attack on the World Trade Center on September 11, 2001. Other dogs helped to locate victims or to find bodies. Information about how dogs are used for arson, customs, and other law enforcement work can be found at <http://www.workingdog.org/>. Invite a K-9 team from local law enforcement agencies to visit your class. Positive reinforcement is used to train the dogs, and the bond between animal and human partners can help students understand compassion. Discuss training techniques and consider reasons why positive reinforcement is better motivation than punishment.

Writing Activity: Police officers take notes about everything that happens and anything suspicious they observe while on duty. Give students small notebooks and have them observe what is happening at school for a few days. Look back to see if anything significant can be discerned from the notes. Did anything interesting or unusual happen at school during that time?

Guest Speaker: Invite a police officer or sheriff's deputy to visit the class. Ask the officer to discuss his or her career, required education and training, and a typical day.

Books to Share:
Andy Russell, NOT Wanted by the Police by David A. Adler.
Cop on the Beat: Officer Steven Mayfield in New York City
    by Arlene Schulman.
Officer Buckle and Gloria by Peggy Rathmann.
The Officers' Ball by Wong Herbert Yee.

Book to Integrate: Criminal Investigation

Case Closed: The Real Scoop on Detective Work by Milton Meltzer.
Meltzer separates the day-to-day work of detectives, crime lab staff, and outside investigators to give real-life examples of criminal investigation work. He includes information on DNA, the Pinkertons, forensic science, and law enforcement agencies.

Career Day: Discuss careers in criminal investigation. Many children are fascinated by television shows that explore forensics. Invite a local criminologist to visit for career day. In addition to private investigators and crime scene investigators, invite artists who sketch crime scenes or develop composite sketches of suspects, lab technicians who work with evidence, computer experts, and others. After the career day (or in lieu of it if your school is not able to schedule speakers), ask each student to pick a job in crime investigation and write a one-page summary of the work involved, the education needed for the job, salary range, and other pertinent information. Gather the summaries and create a career notebook.

Web Resource: The Young Forensic Scientists Forum <http://www.aafs.org/yfsf/index.htm> provides information regarding resources and standards for those interested in careers in forensic science.

Historical Research: Investigate the history of fingerprinting. Although fingerprints were recognized as being unique to each individual as far back as the 14th century, Scotland Yard introduced the first classification system in 1901. Assign students to explore the classification system, fingerprint comparison techniques, collection methodology, and key court cases. Explore new forms of "fingerprinting" that are evolving with new technology. Discuss whether fingerprints are still important crime fighting tools today when DNA and other tools are available. Can two people have the same DNA? What is a DNA fingerprint?

Web Resource: The FBI offers information about fingerprint identification at <http://www.fbi.gov/kids/>. Beginning in 1924 with 810,188 fingerprints, the files have now grown to more than 250 million sets of prints. They receive over 34,000 fingerprints every day.

Figure 5.3: Fingerprint Characters Illustration

Art: Create fingerprint characters. Gather colored inkpads, white paper, colored pencils or thin-line markers, and moist towelettes (for cleaning fingers). Have children use their fingers and thumbs to make prints. Add features like eyes, mouths, hands, and legs with pencils or markers. Books like Ed Emberley's *Complete Funprint Drawing Book* also offer examples and inspiration.

Biography: Learn about the Pinkerton company's history and find information about Allan Pinkerton at <http://www.pinkertons.com/>. The Library of Congress also has photographs at <http://rs6.loc.gov/ammem/today/aug25.html>. Make a list of interesting facts about Pinkerton. What cases did he solve? The agency's logo and slogan, "the All-Seeing Eye," inspired the phrase "Private Eye," and Pinkerton's work to prevent the assassination of President Lincoln led to the formation of the U.S. Secret Service. What does the Secret Service do today?

Guest Speaker: Invite a private investigator to visit the class and discuss the kinds of work being done today by private eyes. Create a list comparing reality with fictional or television detectives. Students can think up a name for their own detective agency and develop a logo and slogan. Use the template provided to create a door hanger for the agency (or use a die-cut machine to create door hangers).

Books to Share:
Allan Pinkerton: The Original Private Eye by Judith Pinkerton Josephson.
The Bone Detectives: How Forensic Anthropologists Solve Crimes and Uncover Mysteries of the Dead by Donna Jackson.
Fingerprints and Talking Bones: How Real-Life Crimes are Solved by Charlotte Foltz Jones.
Police Lab: How Forensic Science Tracks Down and Convicts Criminals by David Owen.
Secret Service by Mark Beyer.
Solving Crimes: Pioneers of Forensic Science by Ron Fridell.

Figure 5.4: Door Hanger Pattern

History

Book to Integrate: Ancient Egypt

The 5,000-Year-Old Puzzle by Claudia Logan.
When King Tut's tomb was uncovered in 1922, everyone wanted to know what it contained. Logan uses a fictional boy to allow readers to follow along on the expedition as the archeologists uncover the mysteries of Ancient Egypt.

Writing Activity: In *The 5,000-Year-Old Puzzle*, the hieroglyphs have to be deciphered to identify the owner of the tomb. The translation provides hints about the owner's identity before revealing her name. Talk about how each student would identify himself or herself without using his or her name. For example, "She who lives with cats" and "Follower of Dewey" would be descriptors for the author of this book.

Geography: Place a map of Egypt on a bulletin board. Ask students to mark locations where mummies have been found. Start with Giza and Cairo, and see what other towns or areas the students can locate.

Fun Facts: Students can search for pictures of Egypt on the Internet, in old magazines (many people will donate old issues of *National Geographic*), or in travel brochures. Each student should use pictures and index cards to make a postcard. Students will write a few facts about whatever is shown in the selected picture. For example, if the picture is of the Great Sphinx, the student might write: "The body of the Sphinx is 240 feet long." Place the postcards in clear plastic sleeves in a notebook so that everyone can enjoy the pictures and facts.

Art: Students will make their own cartouches. Cartouches are hieroglyphics versions of a name, placed in an oval ring. Print out the oval cartouche pattern and ask students to use the symbols provided to create their names in the cartouche. Use James Rumford's book *Seeker of Knowledge: The Man Who Deciphered Egyptian Hieroglyphs* as an additional resource.

Culture: Talk about what other items were put in tombs with the mummies. Ask students to list the items they would want with them. For details of mummification, use Aliki's *Mummies Made in Egypt* or James M. Deem's *Bodies From the Bog*.

Guest Speaker: Invite an archeologist or Egyptologist to visit the class. Ask that person to bring some Egyptian artifacts to show the class. If there is a museum nearby, plan a class trip. Visit the British Museum's Egypt Room online at <http://www.ancientegypt.co.uk/menu.html> for interactive experiences related to Ancient Egypt, mummification, writing, artifacts, and more.

Web Resource: Canon provides templates for 3-D models of the Sphinx and the Great Pyramid at <http://bj.canon.co.jp/english/3D-papercraft/building/index05.html>.

> **Books to Share:**
> *The Egypt Game* by Zilpha Keatley Snyder.
> *Mummies in the Morning* by Mary Pope Osborne.
> *Mummy Mysteries from North America* by Brenda Z. Guiberson.
> *Mystery of the Whispering Mummy* by Robert Arthur.
> *Secrets of the Pyramids: a Maze Adventure* by Graham White.

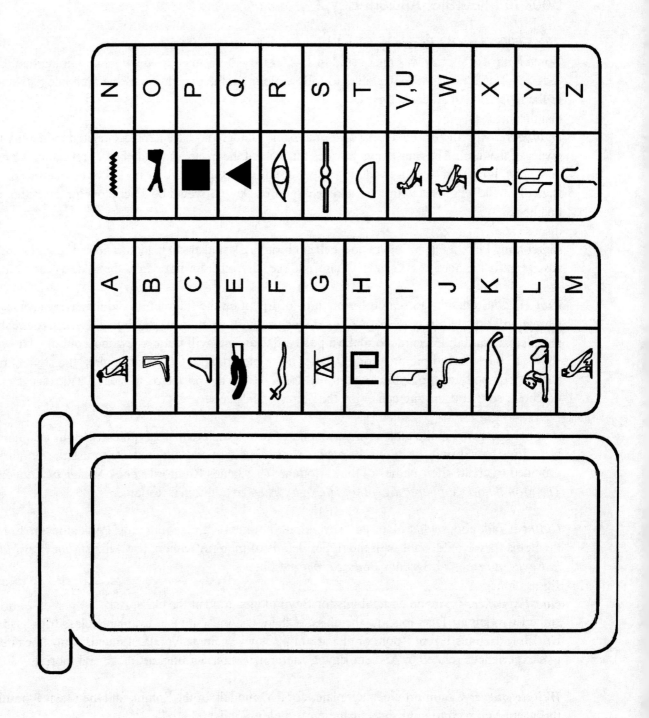

Figure 5.5: Cartouche Pattern

Book to Integrate: Secrets

There's a Dead Person Following My Sister Around by Vivian Vande Velde.
Although he thinks he lives in an ordinary house, the ghost of an African-American slave is shadowing Ted's five-year-old sister. The discovery of a diary provides the clues needed to solve the problem.

Creative Writing: Ted is told that one of his ancestors was "the black sheep of the family." He knows that this means "somebody nobody wanted to admit being related to." Work with the class to come up with samples of other idioms that use animals to describe people, personal relationships, or characteristics. Ask each student develop one example of his or her own creation.

Architecture: Grandma tells Ted to write about the secret room. Look at the houses in your neighborhood. Could the modern houses have a secret room? Look at books on architecture and discuss some of the styles that more readily lend themselves to secret rooms and hidden passages. Why are some styles better than others for hiding places?

Historical Research: Ted finds a journal from 1850. Use the Internet, encyclopedias, newspapers on microfilm, or other reference sources to find something that happened in your community (or elsewhere) in 1850. Have students keep journals for a few weeks. Discuss how entries written today about commonplace events might provide useful information 100 years from now.

> ***Books to Share:***
> *Baby-sitting is a Dangerous Business* by Willo Davis Roberts.
> *Christina's Ghost* by Betty Ren Wright.
> *False Face* by Welwyn Wilton Katz.
> *House of Dies Drear* by Virginia Hamilton.
> *Skelton Man* by Joseph Bruchac.

Book to Integrate: Holidays

The Case of the Secret Valentine by James Preller.
Jigsaw Jones, a second-grade detective, is receiving mysterious valentines and each card offers a clue. By solving the secret codes, Jones is able to crack the case.

Compare and Contrast: Research how Valentine's Day started. List the things Jigsaw likes (he gets cupcakes) and does not like (the mushy stuff) about the holiday.

Writing Activity: Jigsaw Jones keeps a journal of his activities. Ask students to keep journals of their activities for at least a month.

Music: Mila makes up a Valentine's song and sings it to the tune of "The Farmer in the Dell." Using a familiar tune with new lyrics is called a "piggyback" song and provides an easy writing experience. Write lyrics about your favorite mystery or detective.

Art: Mysteries are like jigsaw puzzles—you need all of the pieces to see the whole picture. Ask each student to draw a picture (or use photographs from old magazines) of something mysterious. Glue the picture to cardboard and cut into pieces. Place the pieces in an envelope and give to another student to put together.

> ***Books to Share:***
> *Albert's Halloween* by Leslie Tryon.
> *Aunt Eater's Mystery Halloween* by Doug Cushman.
> *The Bear Detectives* by Stan Berenstain and Jan Berenstain.
> *Nate the Great and the Crunchy Christmas* by Marjorie Weinman Sharmat.
> *Nursery Crimes* by Arthur Geisert.

Book to Integrate: Birthdays

Cam Jansen and the Birthday Mystery by David A. Adler.
Cam's surprise birthday party for her parents almost turns to disaster when her grandparents have their luggage stolen. Fortunately, Cam's photographic memory provides the critical clue.

Memory Exercise: Talk about what it means to have a photographic memory. Does it really exist? (See <http://www.straightdope.com/columns/000901.html> for an article by Cecil Adams.) True photographic memory probably does not exist, but we can train our memory through exercises. List names on the board and give students one minute to memorize it. Cover the names and ask the students to write down as many names as they can remember. What does it mean when Cam says "Click"? How do we help ourselves remember important things?

Compare and Contrast: List the ways we celebrate our birthdays. Use a book like *Birthdays Around the World* by Mary Lankford to learn how birthdays are celebrated in other countries and cultures. Compare and contrast things like party games, food, gifts, and so on. Research traditions in countries not included in this book.

Vocabulary Builder: Mnemonics are techniques that help us remember dates, names, facts, and such. Some popular mnemonics include "spring forward, fall back" for daylight savings time, "i before e—except after c" for spelling help, or "In 1492 Columbus sailed the ocean blue" to remember historical dates. Use the database at <http://www.eudesign.com/mnems/> to locate mnemonics to share with the class, and then ask students to think of some new ones.

Book to Integrate: Feuds

The Coffin Quilt: The Feud Between the Hatfields and the McCoys by Ann Rinaldi.
Fanny McCoy lives with the age-old feud between her family and the Hatfield family in the mountains of Kentucky. In the midst of killing and revenge, Fanny is the only voice of reason when her sister runs off to marry Johnse Hatfield.

Research: Discuss the meaning of "feud." Talk about why feuds start and how they sometimes continue for so long that people do not remember what they were arguing about. Find examples of famous feuds. The Hatfields and McCoys feuded for more than a century, but other well-known feuds occurred between singers Sonny and Cher, lawman Wyatt Earp and the Clinton brothers, and political figures Aaron Burr and Alexander Hamilton. Use library reference materials to find out what these feuds were about.

Vocabulary Builder: It is sometimes said that there is "bad blood" between people or families that are feuding. List other words that describe animosities (vendetta, ill-will, grudge).

Conflict Resolution: Ask the students to think about conflicts they have seen on the news or in their own lives. Brainstorm to create a list of the ways we can resolve conflicts and avoid animosity. As part of its Choices and Consequences project, Court TV offers videos, curricula, and program guides for classroom use in teaching conflict resolution and tolerance (<http://www.courttv.com/choices/resource.html> or call 877-871-6469).

Historical Connections: In her author notes, Ann Rinaldi notes "the Civil War conditioned men who fought in it to kill and to hate." She hypothesizes that this was one reason for the feud between the Hatfields and the McCoys. What parallels can students find to feuds, violence, and hatred in current events?

Web Resource: A *Life* article on the Hatfields and McCoys, written in 1944, is available online at <http://userwww.service.emory.edu>. Search for additional references to the feud, which, while no longer violent, continues today.

Art: Roseanna sews a coffin quilt, a fabric record of family births and deaths. Have students create paper quilt blocks to record memorable events. You will need six-inch squares of white paper, eight-inch squares of colored paper, crayons or colored pencils, and tape. Each student draws a picture of an occasion in his or her life. Glue the white paper to the colored paper. Tape the squares into a quilt with a row of blank squares for a border. Hang the quilt (or use the squares to create a quilt on the bulletin board by stapling the squares to the board).

> *Books to Share:*
> *Bo & Mzzz Mad* by Sid Fleischman.
> *Sammy Keyes and the Curse of Moustache Mary* by Wendelin Van Draanen.
> *Scribbler of Dreams* by Mary E. Pearson.
> *Shadow-Catcher* by Betty Levin.
> *What Janie Found* by Caroline B. Cooney.

Book to Integrate: Family Histories

The Search for the Shadowman by Joan Lowery Nixon.
Andy's homework assignment requires him to interview a family member in order to write a family history. Great-aunt Winnie's refusal to answer some questions makes Andy curious about his family's secrets.

Interviewing: Genealogists depend on interviews to learn family histories. Ask someone from your local history association to teach basic interview techniques to the class. Develop a list of questions that students will ask a family member. Compile a classroom history book with the stories or put the histories and an appropriate photograph on a classroom Web page.

Personal Safety: Andy does a lot of his research over the Internet. An excellent brochure with tips for kids and parents is available at <http://www.safekids.com/child_safety.htm>. Talk about Internet safety and ask students to write their own rules and discuss safety with their parents.

History: Much of the feud centers around the Texas Salt Wars. Use *The Handbook of Texas* at <http://www.tsha.utexas.edu/handbook/online/> to find out if the war really occurred and what it was about. Why was salt so important to the settlers? Visit the Salt Institute's Web site at <http://www.saltinstitute.org> to learn about the history of salt, how salt is used, and its chemistry. Ask students to find interesting facts about salt (salt was used as currency; a hotel in Bolivia is made entirely out of salt).

Library Research: Andy contacted a reference librarian at the state library to help with his research. Ask students to find out if your state has a state library. Do they offer reference services? Ask the reference librarian from your public library to visit the class and talk about library reference services.

Idea Development: Joan Lowery Nixon said that she found most of the ideas for her novels from common sources like newspaper and magazine articles. When she read something, she would often ask herself "What if?" and then develop a story to answer her own question. Have students read the newspaper and locate articles. List three or four "what if?" questions and write a description of the story that would ensue from the article.

Books to Share:
Burning Up by Caroline B. Cooney.
The Killer's Cousin by Nancy Werlin.
Love Among the Walnuts: Or How I Saved My Entire Family from Being Poisoned by Jean Ferris.
The Moonlight Man by Betty Ren Wright.
The Secret of Gumbo Grove by Eleanora Tate.

Language Arts

Book to Integrate: Poetry

Foreign Exchange: a Mystery in Poems by Mel Glenn.
Pretty, blond, and dead! When Kristen Clarke is found floating in a lake, the prejudices of both urban and rural communities, as well as white middle class versus ethnic poor, start to come to a boil. The mystery unfolds through a series of poems.

Writing Exercise: Cinquain is a form of poetry that uses a five-line stanza of unrhymed words. Review the parts of speech: noun, adjective, verb, synonym, and so on. Then pick a mystery book or character and use the following structure to develop a cinquain.

First line: one word (a noun) that is the subject
Second line: two words (both adjectives) that describe the subject
Third line: three words (all verbs) that give actions
Fourth line: a four- or five-word phrase that tells something about the story
Fifth line: one word that is a synonym for line one or sums up the story

Detective
Observant, Brilliant
Investigating, thinking, sleuthing
The game is afoot!
Holmes.

Activity—Magnetic Words: Ask students to cut interesting words out of old magazines and greeting cards. Glue the words to strips of magnetic tape (available at craft stores) or recycled magnets. Provide a place for the kids to rearrange the words into poetic phrases. Inexpensive cookie sheets work (not aluminum) or buy a small piece of steel sheeting at a home repair store and frame it with colored fabric or duct tape. Be sure to include some mysterious terminology, as well as plenty of articles, adjectives, verbs, and nouns.

> ***Books to Share:***
> *After the Death of Anna Gonzales* by Terri Fields.
> *The Taking of Room 114: A Hostage Drama in Poems* by Mel Glenn.
> *Who Killed Mr. Chippendale?: A Mystery in Poems* by Mel Glenn.

Book to Integrate: Journal Writing

Trial by ~~Jury~~ Journal by Kate Klise.
A new law says that a child must serve on the jury for any case that involves a child victim and Lily Watson is selected. Since she will miss school, she keeps a journal of her experience.

Topic for Discussion: Discuss what a "jury of one's peers" means. Invite a trial lawyer or a court judge to talk about jury duty and why this aspect of the American system of justice is critical to a democratic society.

Art: Each room in the Menagerie Hotel where the jury is sequestered is decorated like a different animal. Ask each student to decide what animal they would like to have a room decorated like. Students should then draw a picture or make a diorama.

> ***Books to Share:***
> *Ghost of Fossil Glen* by Cynthia DeFelice.
> *Letters From Camp* by Kate Klise.
> *The Mystery of Mineral Gorge* by Julia Van Nutt.
> *Regarding the Fountain: a Tale, in Letters, of Liars and Leaks*
>   by Kate Klise.
> *Serving on a Jury* by Sarah De Capua.

Book to Integrate: Wacky Words

The Missing Mummy by Ron Roy.
Dink, Josh, and Ruth Rose visit the museum to see a child mummy in an actual tomb. However, the mummy has been stolen and the kids have to unravel the mystery to return the mummy to the exhibit.

Vocabulary Builder: Writers spend a lot of time on vocabulary, searching to find the perfect word to describe their thoughts. Ask students to listen and look for words that deal with mysteries, crime, or criminal justice and keep a notebook of words to incorporate into a mystery.

Word Play: The museum offers special events for children each day of the week. Mummy Monday, Tyrannosaurus Tuesday, Wet Wednesday, and so on. Ask the children to think about events that your school or library could do (use days of the week and months) and make up alliterative phrases for each. For example, Nutty November could be a month of silly activities; Tasty Tuesday could be a day for special food treats. As a group, decide on one special day and develop ideas for activities, food, and fun for that day.

Book to Integrate: Tough Talk

Tough Cookie by David Wisniewski.
Tough Cookie is a rough-talking, trench coat-wearing private eye and his life is crumbling around him. This clever spoof is filled with puns and fun.

Similes: Tough Cookie is considered "noir-ish." Discuss Wisniewski's play on words, talk about what "noir" means in literature, and what makes this book "noir-ish." Look at some of the phrases he uses, like "A slap stings my cheek like a velvet bee." Discuss the meaning of this simile and ask the students to make up additional sayings.

Writing Activity: The characters and criminal gangs are all named for cookies, like Pecan Sandy and the Ginger Snaps. Let the students make up characters based on their favorite cookies. Write out descriptions for each new character. For example, what would Hy Drox or Chips A'Hoy look like? How do they behave and what are their characteristics?

Art: David Wisniewski used an art technique that layers cut paper shapes to create the picture. For younger students, provide them with an assortment of pre-cut paper shapes and glue sticks to create their own picture. Older students can cut their own shapes.

Sample Lesson Outlines

Personal Safety

Subjects: Vocabulary, writing, social studies, art
Grades: First through third
Purpose: To discuss personal safety, the effects of bullying and violence, and ways to avoid gangs and criminal activities.

Book to Integrate: *The Berenstain Bears and No Guns Allowed* by Jan Berenstain and Stan Berenstain. For a class assignment, Ferdy and Too-Tall look at the invention of the gun. It quickly becomes apparent that Too-Tall's interest is not academic and problems ensue when he brings in a very realistic looking squirt gun.

Discussion: Read *The Berenstain Bears and No Guns Allowed*. Begin a discussion about the culture of violence and the differences between fantasy (playing "cops and robbers") and reality (school violence, Columbine High School, bullying). It is usually better to discuss these subjects before a problem occurs, but, if there have been incidents of violence at your school, quality literature and discussion can help children heal.

Vocabulary Builder: What is a clique? How do cliques differ from gangs, clubs, or other groups? Talk about unacceptable and inappropriate behavior (no guns, bullying, being rude, taking something that is not yours, cussing) and inclusiveness.

Art: Give students poster board and art supplies and allow them to create signs and posters that encourage appropriate behavior, kindness, and inclusiveness.

Civics: Mama Bear and some of the other mothers sign a petition to ask the video store to label violent movies so that parents would know which videos were not appropriate. Talk about petitions and how people can influence public opinion or effect change. If the students determine that there is a need for change in the school, see if the principal will permit them to circulate a petition, perhaps to eliminate name-calling at school.

Celebration: Although safety is a year-round issue, use School Safety Month in October to focus reading and activities on personal safety, eliminating violence, and security. The National Center for Missing and Exploited Children <http://www.missingkids.com> has brochures and information on school and neighborhood safety and online quizzes.

Discussion: Talk about why kids join gangs and brainstorm ways to avoid getting involved with a gang. How is a club different from a gang? List descriptors and ask the students to list strategies for being involved in positive experiences rather than dangerous and inappropriate activities.

> **Additional Reading:**
> *Smoky Night* by Eve Bunting.
> *Don't Talk to Strangers* by Kevi.
> *Stars in the Darkness* by Barbara Joosse.

Dangers of the Sea

Subjects: History, science, ecology, geography, cartography, folklore
Grades: Fourth through sixth
Purpose: To discover the wonders and dangers of sea life and the history and folklore of piracy.

Book to Integrate: *The Coral Coffin* by Michael Dahl. Finn Zwake and his grandfather, a famous mystery writer, are swept overboard during an expedition to Australia's Great Barrier

Reef. They drift ashore on a deserted island where they find a dead body—and pirates. Rescued by the pirates, the duo is accused of poisoning the crew one-by-one. Finn has to figure out who is responsible for the dastardly deeds in order to save himself and his grandfather.

Scientific Theory: Occam's Razor is mentioned several times in this book. This scientific principle suggests that we "keep it simple." Given several possible theories, we are encouraged not to make complicated assumptions but to pursue the simplest answers first. Use Occam's Razor to examine the evidence that Finn sees in this book.

Research—Coral Reefs and Sea Creatures: Look on the Internet or in books to find out what a geography cone looks like. What other creatures can your students identify that are poisonous to people?

Talk about coral reefs. Where else are there reefs? Why are they in danger and what can we do to help maintain the reefs? Look at *Mother Jones* magazine's Web site at <http://www.motherjones.com/coral_reef/> for a map of reef locations and some information on the plight of reefs around the world.

Craft: Make a ship in a bottle. Each child needs a sheet of deep blue construction paper, brown construction paper, white paper (light weight), a sheet of white tagboard or heavy construction paper, scissors, glue sticks, clear plastic food wrap, and tape. Trace the ship pattern on blue construction paper and on brown construction paper. Trace the sails pattern on white paper. Cut out each pattern. Glue the bottle to the white tagboard. Glue the ship in the center of the bottle, leaving a small opening in the center for the ship's mast. Use white crayons to make a few waves around the ship. Punch holes in the sail and thread a short length of drinking straw through the holes. Glue the end of the straw under the loose edge of the ship and press down. Measure plastic wrap larger than the construction paper. Stretch the plastic wrap over the whole thing, taping the plastic wrap on the back to give the effect of glass.

History Research: Pirates hold Finn and his grandfather captive. Research historical pirates, including Captain Kidd, Blackbeard, Jean Lafitte, and Henry Morgan; do not forget female pirates like Mary Reed and Anne Bonny. Pirates were and still are dangerous; discuss some of the reasons we are fascinated by their exploits. Read Jane Yolen's *Ballad of the Pirate Queens* for information on female pirates. Read aloud or listen to an audiobook production of *Treasure Island* by Robert Louis Stevenson.

Craft Activity: Give children a copy of the Jolly Roger flag pattern and ask them to design their own Jolly Roger. Talk about the traditional skull and crossbones. What did it signify? Ask each student to think about what is significant or important to him or her. What do you want your flag to say about you? Design the flag to represent a personal interest.

Vocabulary Builder: The pirate captain's name is Blue Jade. Talk about why she was named that and then have students develop their own colorful pirate names. How is the word "pirate" used today? Talk about why "pirating" software or music is illegal.

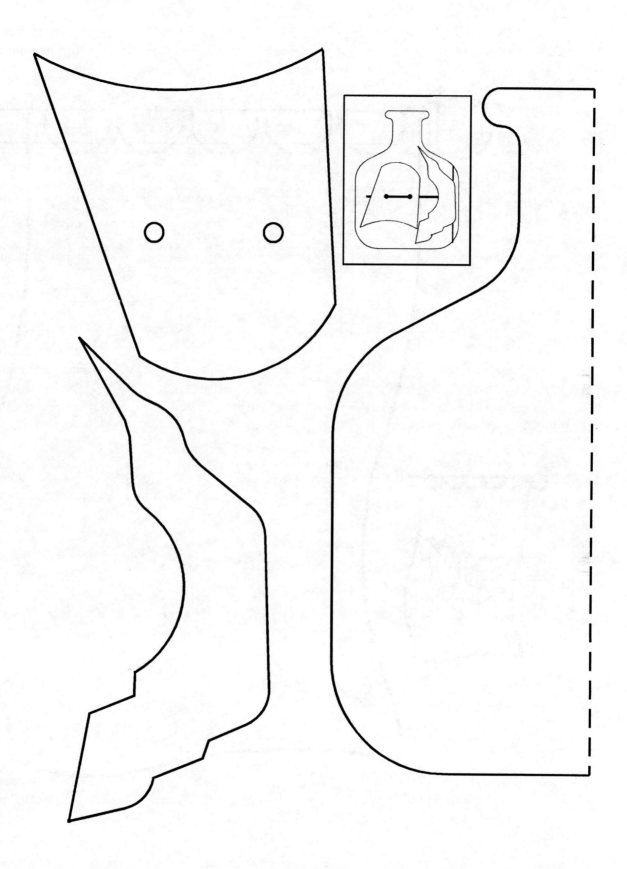

Figure 5.6: Ship in a Bottle Pattern

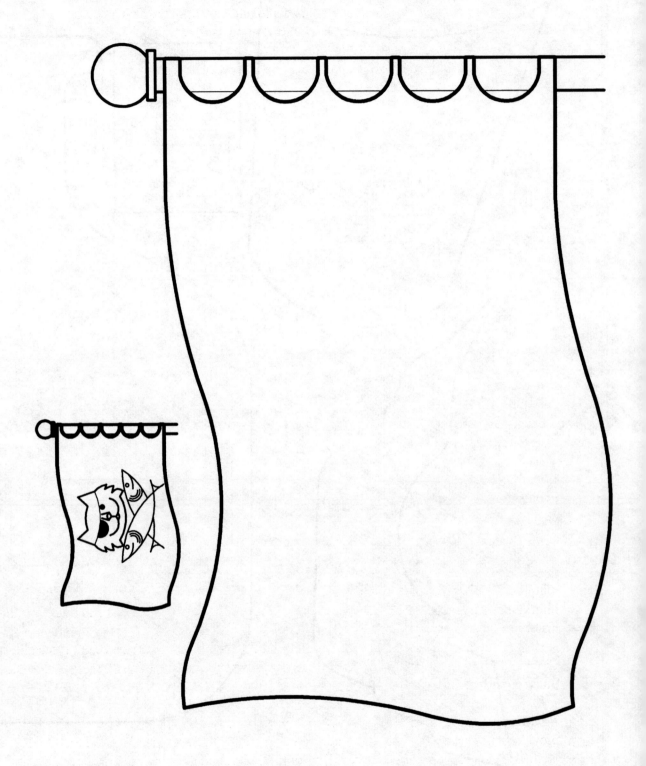

Figure 5.7: Jolly Roger Flag Pattern

- Historical information and activities related to pirates is available at <http://www.nationalgeographic.com/features/97/pirates/maina.html>.
- The Virtual World Great Barrier Reef at <http://www.nationalgeographic.org> offers a virtual tour of Australia's Great Barrier Reef and the animals that live in that area.
- The National Oceanic and Atmospheric Administration (NOAA) provides information at <http://www.coralreef.noaa.gov>.

Cartography: Maps are important to seafarers. Use a world map and trace the probable route that Finn and his grandfather took to get from Iceland to the Great Barrier Reef.

Film Resource: Pirates of the Barbary Coast.

Additional Reading:
The Book of Pirates by Howard Pyle.
The Not-So-Jolly Roger by Jon Scieszka.
Pirates Past Noon by Mary Pope Osborne.
The Pirates of Pompeii by Caroline Lawrence.

In the Footsteps of Sherlock Holmes

Subjects: Literature, geography, history, mathematics, art, writing
Grades: Fifth through eighth
Purpose: To explore the literary work of Sir Arthur Conan Doyle and discover the world of Victorian England.

Classroom Reading: Favorite Sherlock Holmes Detective Stories is available from Dover Publications. This low cost edition is perfect for classroom sets. Pick any of the eight stories to read as a group or assign different stories to groups of students.

Cartography: Have students use a map of the London Underground (subway) to locate some of the places mentioned in the Sherlock Holmes stories they read. The Web site at <http://www.thetube.com/> offers printable maps of the subway system as well as extensive information on London. Look at subway stops for major London attractions and museums, the history of the subway system, and descriptions of "ghost" stations (stations that are out of service or no longer exist). Pinpoint some of the places that Holmes and Watson went (Piccadilly Circus, Charing Cross Station, Baker Street) as well as modern attractions (Abbey Road, BBC Studios, Guinness Book of World Records).

Web Resource: The Sherlockian Atlas at <http://www.evo.org/sherlock/sherlock_atlas.html> provides an index and Concordia of all geographical locations mentioned in the Sherlock Holmes canon. Organized geographically, by story title, and alphabetically, a clickable map allows readers to quickly determine whether a location is real or fictional and learn more about the location. In some cases, users may even view photographs of the area.

Math: Use the timetables for the London Underground to calculate the how long it would take

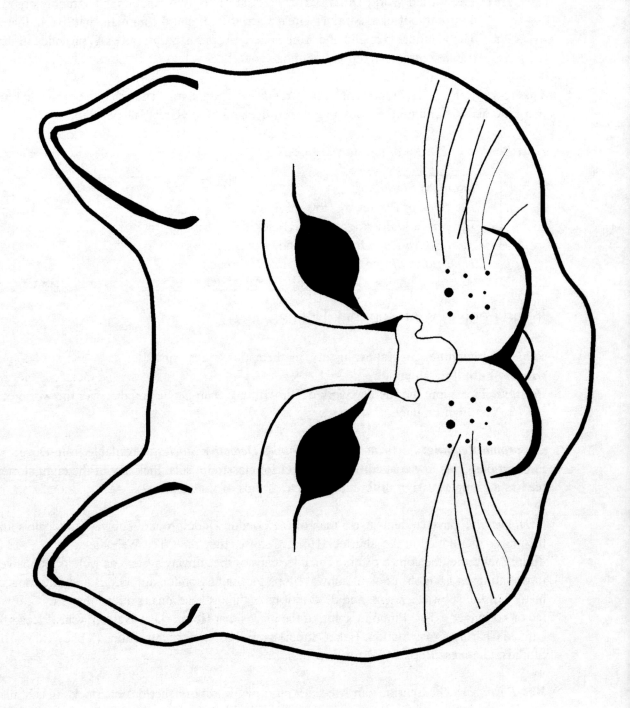

Figure 5.8: Mystery Cat Pattern

for Holmes and Watson to reach their destinations. What would it cost today to make the trip? The prices are provided in British pounds, so students need to find a currency converter to calculate the price in U.S. dollars. Based on the rate of inflation since Holmes' time, ask students to calculate what it would have cost the detective to travel.

Art: There was no building at 221-B Baker Street, although today there is a museum specifically placed at that address. Look at photographs of the museum, descriptions of Holmes' house in the stories, and descriptions found in other books about Holmes. Students can draw a room layout, create a diorama, or paint their interpretation of this famous house.

Writing Activity: Even though he is a fictional character, many people write to Sherlock Holmes at 221-B Baker Street and the post office delivers the mail. Ask students to write a letter to Holmes or Watson asking questions about how a case was solved or requesting assistance on a new case.

Poetry: Use the pattern provided to photocopy a mask outline for each student. Read T.S. Eliot's poem, "Macavity the Mystery Cat" from *Old Possum's Book of Practical Cats,* and then ask each student to create his or her own "Napoleon of Crime." List Macavity's crimes as they are tallied in the poem. See if students can find the allusions and references to other Sherlock Holmes mysteries included in the poem. Eliot's poetry was the inspiration for the Broadway musical, *Cats.* Develop a scene based on this poem and act it out.

Creative Thinking: Sir Arthur Conan Doyle tried to kill off his popular character when he tired of writing the stories. Bowing to popular pressure, he had to figure out how to bring Holmes back from the grave. Read "The Final Problem" and then have students list their ideas for how Holmes might have escaped death.

Research: Scotland Yard plays an important role in the Sherlock Holmes stories. Research the history of this organization. Why is it called Scotland Yard? When was it formed and what historical cases have been solved by Scotland Yard? Information is available at the Metropolitan Police Web site <http://www.met.police.uk/index.shtml>, especially in the history section and its links.

Film Resource: Sherlock Holmes, the Great Detective.

Audiovisual Resources:
- Sherlock Holmes Radio Mysteries. Countertop Audio, 2002. A new series of radio broadcasts from the BBC is available on audiocassette.
- Sherlock Holmes Consulting Detective, 1999. A DVD interactive video allows players to match wits with Holmes as they solve three cases.

Additional Reading:
The Adventures of Sherlock Holmes by Sir Arthur Conan Doyle.
The Case of the Baker Street Irregular by Robert Newman.
Freddy the Detective by Walter Brooks.
Match Wits with Sherlock Holmes: The Adventures of the Dancing Men
   by Murray Shaw.
Trouble in Bugland: A Collection of Inspector Mantis Mysteries
   by William Kotzwinkle.

Additional Curriculum Ideas

Vocabulary Builders: Prepare a crossword grid that is at least 10 squares by 10 squares (use graph paper or simply create a table using a word processing program). Ask students to create crossword puzzles with vocabulary words from a mystery they have read. Each student should begin by creating a list of words. Then the students begin to fill in the blanks on a grid. Make sure that at least one letter connects through the words, that the words run only across from left to right or down the page, and that each word is only used once. Students may find that they cannot use all of their words in the puzzle. For each word used, the student should write a clue. Make copies of the crossword puzzles and duplicate them for other students to solve. Create crossword puzzles online at <http://www.edhelper.com/wordfind.htm>. Put in words, add clues, and a crossword puzzle is developed to print out.

Creative Writing: Use pictures books to help students understand the structure of a mystery. Read several simple mysteries so that students understand plot, tension, character, and resolution. As a group, decide on the detective, the criminal, the crime to be committed, and the location of the crime.

Most mystery stories look at means, motive, and opportunity. Answer these questions to get the story started:

- Who is the victim and who are the suspects? (opportunity)
- What was the crime?
- Where was the crime committed?
- Why was the crime committed? (motive)
- How was the crime committed? (means)

Starting with the same information, each student will write his or her own short story mystery. Read the stories aloud and discuss how each writer came up with a different story, and solution, from similar information. Books like *Writing Mysteries, Movies, Monster Stories, and More* by Nancy Bentley and Donna Guthrie or *How to Write a Story* by Kathleen C. Phillips can help students understand dialogue, plot, setting, and other required elements.

Who Dun It?: Create a reading list of books that you would like students to read. The list can include any kinds of books (no need to limit yourself to mysteries), but do not include the author's name. Instead, challenge the students to find out "Who Dun It?" Distribute copies of the list and ask students to fill in the author's name and the library call number as they search for the answers.

Audio Resource: Edgar Allan Poe's Stories and Tales II. Monterey Soundworks, 2000. Full-cast performances provide faithful adaptations of Poe's classic tales.

Journalism: Read a mystery and then write a headline for a newspaper article that will tell the story. Remember that headlines are less than 10 words! The headlines can be straightforward (think *New York Times*) or sensational (like the *National Enquirer*). For example, a headline for *The Dollhouse Murders* might read, "Dolls Solve 50-Year-Old Puzzle" or "Killer Dolls Strike Family."

Mock Trials: *What's the Verdict?: You're the Judge in 90 Tricky Courtroom Quizzes* by Ted LeValliant and Marcel Theroux provides actual cases that can be used for classroom discussions. Each case is depicted in a cartoon-style illustration with a short description of the crime. After discussing the case, the class can learn the verdict, and any appeals, and discuss the issues further. *Jury Trials in the Classroom* by Betty See involves students in the judicial process by staging simulated trials. The author includes three criminal trials and three civil trials featuring characters from literature and history.

Chapter 6

Programming With Mysteries

"Draw your chair up and hand me my violin, for the only problem we have still to solve is how to while away these bleak autumnal evenings" —"The Adventure of the Noble Bachelor"

Programs, whether in public libraries or schools, offer young people the opportunity to enjoy books while having fun. Programming may include book talks or reviews that encourage a kid to try something different. It can include reading aloud, book discussions, reader's theater, and creative dramatics. Many programs include an outside performer or a special guest presenter and often include a craft or another art activity. Programs can focus on one book or on a variety of title—or may not be tied to any specific books. Several programs are provided for mixed-age groups, followed by ideas for specific ages. Use these ideas as starters for your own programs related to mysteries.

Music adds a lot to programming and some great tunes provide a mysterious atmosphere. Purchase *Alfred Hitchcock Presents: Signatures In Suspense* (Hip-O Records, 1999) for a broad selection of music from Hitchcock's major films, *James Bond and Beyond: Classic Themes For Secret Agents* (Spy Guise, 2002) for an assortment of music from film and television, or *100 Greatest TV Themes* (Silva America, 2002) for an assortment of songs that includes many mystery programs.

Suggestions for individual tunes include:

- The theme from "Mission Impossible"
- "Funeral March of a Marionette" (theme from "Alfred Hitchcock Presents")
- The theme from "The Third Man" (also called "The Harry Lime Theme")
- "Harlem Nocturne" (a jazz standard)

Program Outlines

Camp Mystery

> ***Books to Share:***
> *The Camp Knock Knock Mystery* by Betsy Duffey.
> *Nighty-Nightmare* by James Howe.
> *The Summer Camp Mystery* by Gertrude Chandler Warner.

Activity: Tell mystery related jokes and try writing a few. Get inspiration from *The Best Knock-Knock Book Ever* by Charles Keller or the *Biggest Joke Book in the World* by Matt Rissinger and Philip Yates.

Music: Display books and recordings that include favorite camp songs. If someone can play the guitar, Autoharp, or another instrument, invite him or her to participate. Add to the fun by allowing the children to make their own musical instruments; instructions for easy-to-make kazoos, drums, shakers, and such are available in many craft books.

Film Resource: Little Bear: Campfire Tales.

Computer Resource: Arthur's Camping Adventure. The Learning Company, 2000. CD-ROM. Arthur and his classmates go camping and Mr. Ratburn twists his ankle. The players must use deductive reasoning, spatial relationships, and problem-solving skills to lead Arthur and his friends to safety.

Storytelling: Chester tells scary stories in *Nighty Nightmare*, including the terrifying tale of how Bunnicula came to live with the Monroe's. Turn down the lights (use a fake fire if you have one available; otherwise have a few flashlights handy to create a spooky mood), sit in a circle, and tell spooky stories. Try *Familiar and Haunting* by Phillipa Pierce or *The Haunting Hour: Chills in the Dead of Night* by R.L. Stine.

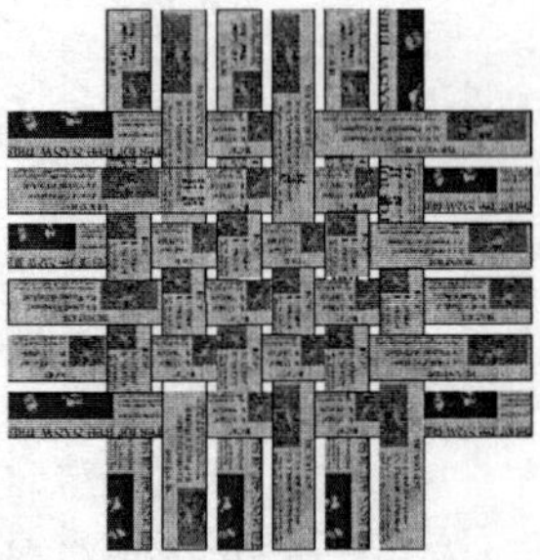

Figure 6.1: Sit-Upon Illustration

Craft: Each participant will make a camp-style "sit-upon" to sit on during programs, at outdoor events, or while camping. For each sit-upon, you will need 10–20 sheets of newspaper (comics or other colored sheets look great!), glue or tape, and clear acrylic spray or clear plastic bags. Fold each sheet from the long edge into the center; continue folding from the outer edge into the center until you have a three-inch strip. Make at least 10 strips (more for larger sizes). Weave the strips over and under, pushing them tightly together. Tuck the ends back into the weaving and glue or tape in place. Spray with an acrylic finish to prevent the ink from rubbing off, or place the sit-upon inside a clear plastic bag and tape closed.

Food: It would not be camp without s'mores! Provide marshmallow, graham crackers, and chocolate squares. Place the marshmallow and chocolate between two graham crackers. Microwave for 30 seconds (test time on your microwave) until the chocolate is soft and the marshmallow is warm.

Wanted!

Books to Share:
Alias by Mary Elizabeth Ryan.
Bad Guys: True Stories of Legendary Gunfighters by Andrew Glass.
The FBI's Most Wanted by Laura D'Angelo.
Wanted ... Mud Blossom by Betsy Byars.

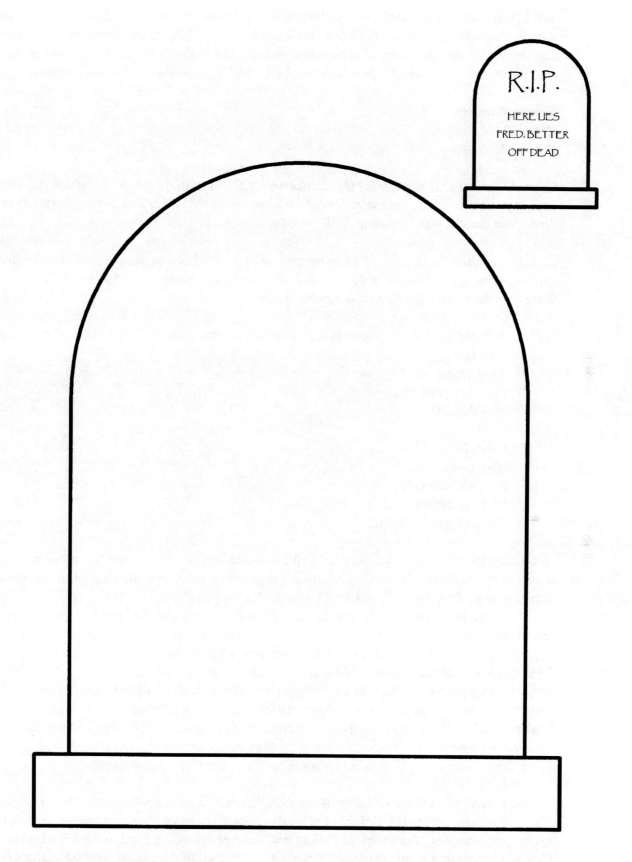

Figure 6.2: Tombstone Pattern

Art: Create "wanted" posters. First, decide on a silly crime (failure to yield the computer, impersonating a giraffe, conspiracy to clown around, and so on). Children can either find pictures in magazines to match the crime or create their own picture of the perpetrator. Paste the pictures onto poster board and add the fugitive's name (the sillier the better!), crime, and reward.

Film Resources:
■ *The Apple Dumpling Gang.*
■ *Dog Day's of the West.*

Craft: Make a sheriff's badge for representatives of the "law in the library." Cut out star shapes from tagboard (most die-cut machines have a star shape available or use any pattern). Let children cover the star with aluminum foil. Glue on a pin back.

Creative Writing: Tombstones contain interesting epitaphs. Look at samples and then let the children write some. Use the pattern provided to reproduce tombstones. Ask the children to write an epitaph. Post the best on the bulletin board.

> Epitaphs can have any format, but many follow this pattern:
> *Here Lies _____*
> *What happened to the person?*
> *The end of this line must rhyme*
> *With this line.*
>
> *Example:*
> *Here Lies Donna,*
> *Too quick with the pen.*
> *Now she edits her book,*
> *From a higher outlook.*

Art: Old gravestones are often very beautiful and rubbings provide an artistic representation of their beauty. To make rubbings, each person needs newsprint or thin drawing paper, fat kindergarten crayons (black or red work well), and masking tape.

Carefully clean away any dirt or moss from the gravestone. Cut paper larger than the area to be rubbed and large enough to protect the gravestone from being marked by the crayon. Tape the paper in place. Use a fat crayon to rub gently across the gravestone with broad strokes. Older students may want to use gold crayons to embellish the rubbing.

Always ask permission to do a rubbing and clean up after yourself. Do not use chalk or other materials that can damage the stones. Do this activity as a group project. A librarian or teacher could do the rubbings to use as decorations. The Association for Gravestone Studies <http://www.gravestonestudies.org/faq.htm> offers advice on how to do rubbings without damaging the headstones, as well as information on the symbolism of gravestones.

Game: Play a "Most Wanted" game by creating "crooks" with the pattern provided. Trace onto tagboard or light cardboard. Color in the shady characters and tape a paperclip to the back of each. Tape a magnet onto a stick or fishing rod. Give each crook a name (Dastardly Dan or Creepy Connie) or a number (Library Enemy #1). Place all of the crooks into the shallow tray and let each child take a turn catching the crooks with the magnet on a stick. Give prizes to those who catch a crook. (For older children, number the crooks and give more points for catching them in order or for catching specific "public enemies.")

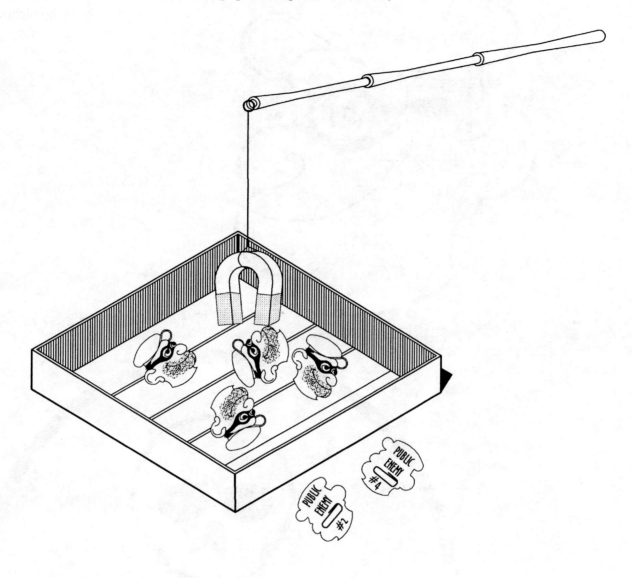

Figure 6.3: Crook Illustration

Hidden Treasure

Books to Share:
The Dark Frigate by Charles Boardman Hawes.
The Erie Canal Pirates by Eric Kimmel.
Ghost Canoe by Will Hobbs.
The Lost Treasure of Captain Kidd by Peter Lourie.
The Mystery of Drear House by Virginia Hamilton.

Figure 6.4: Crook Pattern

Figure 6.5: Skull and
Cross Bone Pattern

Art: Make treasure maps by using parchment paper or brown grocery bags, markers, stencils, scissors, and tea bags. Ask the children to do some research to find out more about Captain Kidd. The University of Massachusetts Amherst has some information on its Web site at <http://www.bio.umass.edu/biology/conn.river/kidd.html>. Have each child draw his or her own treasure map. Use scissors to trim the edges (or tear small pieces off) and then moisten the tea bags and blot on the paper to "age" it (or use ice tea in a spray bottle to lightly spray the paper). Let dry and display.

Food: Purchase gold foil-wrapped coin chocolates and brightly wrapped hard candies (clear peppermints look like diamonds; red, green, and blue wrapped candies look like other jewels). Purchase or make a treasure chest piñata (available at many party stores). Include small carnival beads, rings, and other prizes. Fill the piñata with the candy, hoist it up, and let the children take turns trying to break the treasure chest. If you would rather not use a piñata, simply fill a treasure chest with the candy and let the children grab some loot!

Game: Play a "Find the Treasure!" game by adapting "pin the tail on the donkey." Draw a treasure island on poster paper or newsprint. Mark dangerous areas (sharks off the coast of the island, quicksand pits, a rival band of pirates). Draw the treasure chest. Give each child a skull and cross bones with double stick tape on the back of it. Blindfold each child in turn, spin the child around slowly, and point the pirate toward the treasure. Whoever gets closest to the treasure chest wins a prize.

Action Activity: Play "Walk the Plank." Use a wooden board (a 2 x 4) on the floor for the plank. Each child has to walk the length without falling in. Scatter paper sharks around on the floor for added danger.

Flannel Board Story: Use a pirate character, blue flannel for the ocean, and sea animals. Repeat the rhyme putting different characters on the flannel board. With older children, let them make up lines and create their own flannel board characters.

> *Pirate, Pirate, What Do You See?*
> *Under the waves of the deep blue sea?*
> *I see a shark swimming near me.*

Repeat the first two lines, changing the animals (or other objects) and actions in the third line (I see a treasure chest waiting for me; I see a mermaid beckoning to me; I see an octopus waving at me) to match the flannel pieces you have available.

Poetry: Read "Captain Hook" from Shel Silverstein's *Where the Sidewalk Ends* or "Captain Blackbeard Did" from *A Light in the Attic.*

Film Resources:
■ *The Gold Bug.*
■ *Real McCaw.*

Books to Share:
Aliens in Woodford by Mary Labatt.
The Great Corgiville Kidnapping by Tasha Tudor.
The Great Poochini by Gary Clements.
The Mystery of the Missing Dog by Elizabeth Levy.
Something Queer is Going On by Elizabeth Levy.

Guest Speaker: Invite the local police or sheriff's office to bring a K-9 officer to visit the class or library. Talk about how a dog's great sense of smell helps in investigations. Read books or check out Web sites to learn about the dogs used in criminal investigations. The FBI has interesting information and facts about various dogs at its kid's site <http://www.fbi.gov/kids/dogs/doghome.htm>.

Craft: Make K-9 trading cards. Gather pictures of dogs (from magazines or discarded books), index cards, glue sticks, scissors, and pens. Cut out pictures of dogs and glue to the front of an index card. Use the back to write highlights about the dog's features: breed, age, weight, type of work. If your local law enforcement agency has a K-9 unit, take photographs of those dogs and interview the officers about their dogs' achievements to create trading cards.

Community Service: Pennies to Protect Police Dogs is an organization that raises funds to purchase bulletproof vests for police dogs in many states. A 10-year-old girl started this charity in 2002. See if

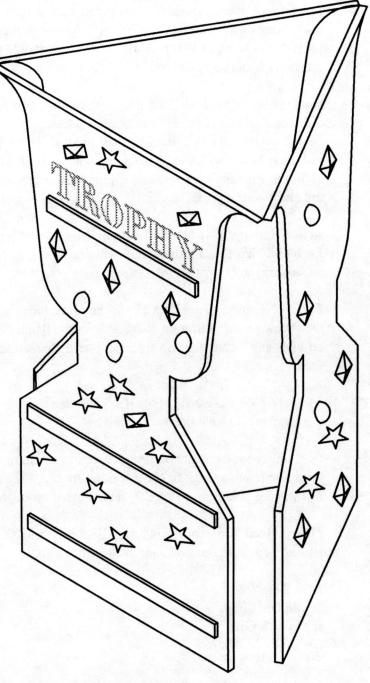

Figure 6.6: Fletcher's Trophy Illustration

the police department (or sheriff's department) in your area needs vests (each costs about $600) or other supplies for their canine officers, or raise funds to send to this organization.

Craft: Read *Something Queer is Going On* or another book about a dog that helps solve a crime. Use the pattern on page 74 (or a die-cut machine) to cut out a trophy on heavy paper for each child. Provide glue sticks, gold foil, glitter, star stickers, and paint pens and let the children prepare a trophy for their favorite crime-solving canine. Fold on the dotted lines and tape to make it stand up. As an alternative activity, if your community has K-9 officers, the children could make trophies to present to those dogs.

Food: Make *Puppy Chow* in advance or at the beginning of the program to serve after it has cooled.

Ingredients:
1/2 cup plain peanut butter
1/2 cup margarine
6 oz chocolate chips
1 box dry cereal (Corn Chex, Cheerios, Crispix)
2 cups powdered sugar

Melt margarine and chocolate chips in a saucepan over medium heat or in a microwave. Add the peanut butter and stir until melted and mixed. Put the cereal in a large mixing bowl. Pour the melted chocolate and peanut butter over the cereal; stir until all the cereal is coated. Put two cups powdered sugar in a large paper grocery bag. Put cereal mixture into the bag and shake gently until all cereal is coated. Pour out on wax paper or a tray to cool. Serve in a plastic dog food bowl or put into plastic "doggy bags" for the children to take home (if food is not permitted in the library).

I Spy!

Books to Share:
Adam Sharp: London Calling by George Edward Stanley.
The Amazing Life of Moe Berg: Catcher, Scholar, Spy
    by Tricia Andryszewski.
Gay-Neck: The Story of a Pigeon by Dhan Gopal Mukerji.
Howie Bowles, Secret Agent by Kate Banks.
I Was a Third Grade Spy by Mary Jane Auch.

Creative Writing: Ask the children to write short descriptions of themselves as spies and pick an alias. Kids should consider how they would change their look and what mannerisms might give away their identity.

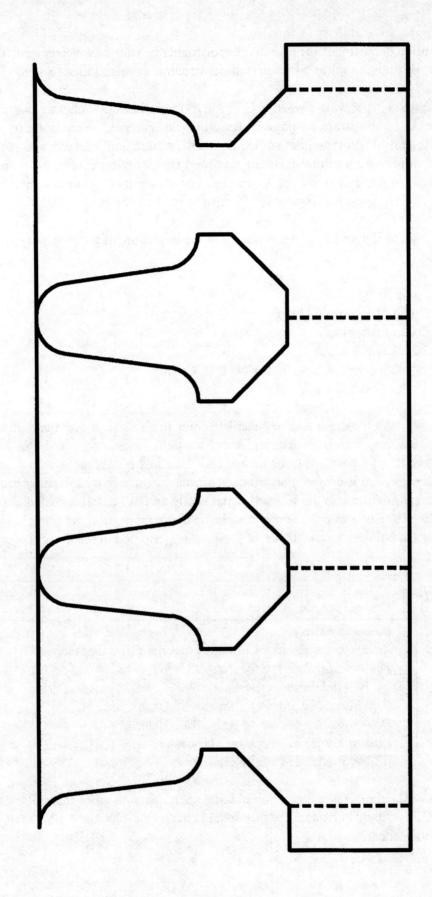

Figure 6.7: Fletcher's Trophy Pattern

Creative Dramatics: Provide materials for participants to create disguises. Hats, wigs, scarves, make-up, glasses, and such are perfect for costume development.

Guest Speaker: Carrier pigeons were used to send secret messages in early Roman times, during the Civil War, and even until recently in India. Although pigeons are no longer needed to send messages, invite a member of a racing pigeon club to bring in a bird and talk about the sport. The National Pigeon Association <http://www.npausa.com> or the American Racing Pigeon Union <http://www.pigeon.org> can help locate groups in your area.

Film Resources:
■ *Harriet the Spy.*
■ *Spy Kids.*

Craft: Spies develop a lot of tools to help them hide secrets, get into places they should not go, and avoid being caught. Talk about far-fetched tools used by movie spies (Maxwell Smart's shoe phone, James Bond's invisible car). Provide children with an assortment of craft materials, including nuts, bolts, aluminum foil, plastic containers, and craft sticks. See what prototypes for new spy equipment each child can create. Display the results.

Web Resource: The International Spy Museum in Washington, D.C., provides information on infamous spies, a glossary of espionage lingo, online games, and other resources at <http://www.spymuseum.org>.

Demonstration: Many communities have security companies or "spy" stores. Invite the manager to bring in surveillance equipment and demonstrate how the items are used. Ask the person to talk about illegal surveillance and privacy laws in your community.

Craft: Spies need passports to be able to move from country to country. Provide each child with several sheets of paper and a copy of the passport cover pattern. If possible, print the cover on heavy copy paper that is brown or antiqued to provide a "leather" look. Use a digital camera or Polaroid to take a picture of each participant. Staple the passport pages between the cover. Use rubber stamps that represent countries or stickers with flags from various countries to "validate" the passport after the participant's fill in the facts about that country.

Private Eye

> ***Books to Share:***
> *The High-Rise Private Eye: The Case of the Puzzling Possum*
>   by Cynthia Rylant.
> *Casebook of a Private (Cat's) Eye* by Mary Stolz.
> *Janie's Private Eye* by Zilpha Keatley Snyder.
> *Marty Frye, Private Eye* by Janet Tashijian.

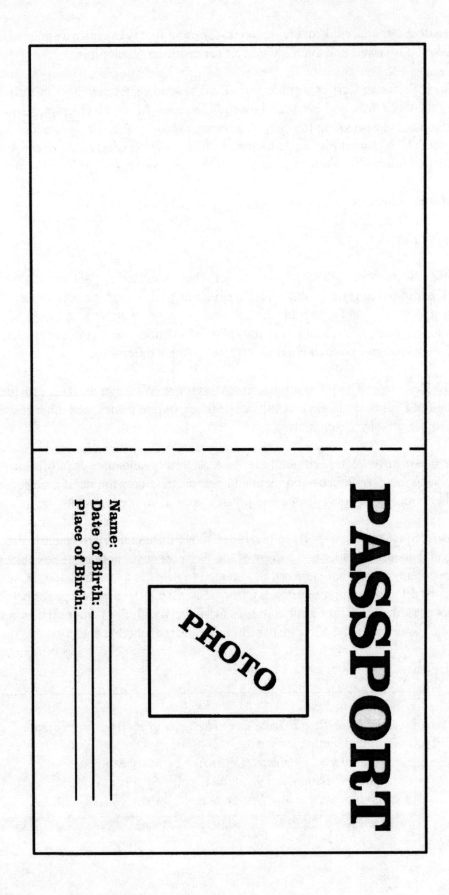

Figure 6.8: Passport Cover Pattern

Creative Thinking: What's in a name? Choose a favorite detective and give clues to his or her personality based only on the letters in his or her name. List the first or last name vertically on a piece of paper. Think of adjective that begins with each letter and describes the detective.

H: Helpful

O: Observant

L: Loyal

M: Moral

E: Excitable

S: Smart

Activity: A detective has to be very observant and pay attention to details. Test the children's powers of observation by gathering about two-dozen small objects (key, safety pin, playing card, small toy) and placing them on a tray. Cover the tray with a towel. Distribute paper and pencils to the players. Remove the towel and give the players one minute to look at the items. Cover the tray again. Players have two minutes to write down as many of the items as they can remember. Give one point for each item recalled. Was anyone able to remember specific details? For example, what suit was the playing card? Was the safety pin open or closed? What kind of toy?

Puzzle Competition: Gather enough jigsaw puzzles to hold a competition. All of the puzzles should have the same number of pieces and be of similar difficulty. Group the participants in teams of two to four. First prize goes to the team that completes the puzzle the fastest or the team that gets the most done within one hour. Play mysterious music and serve snacks during the competition.

Craft: Every detective needs a notebook, magnifying glass, hat, and camera. Provide the raw materials for each child to make a detective kit. Cut out a circle (or use a die-cut machine) for the magnifying glass. Cover with clear cellophane to give the effect of glass. Tape to a craft stick or use brown cardboard to make a handle. To make a notebook use white paper cut to 3" by 5" size. Each child gathers 12–15 sheets of paper and staples them together. Use colored index cards for the front and back. Each detective should decorate the front of his or her notebook. For a hat, copy the Deerstalker Hat pattern for each child to color or decorate. Attach a strip of paper long enough to create a band around the child's head. Staple or tape to the sides of the hat to fit snugly.

Film Resource: *Encyclopedia Brown, the Boy Detective, in The Case of the Amazing Race Car.*

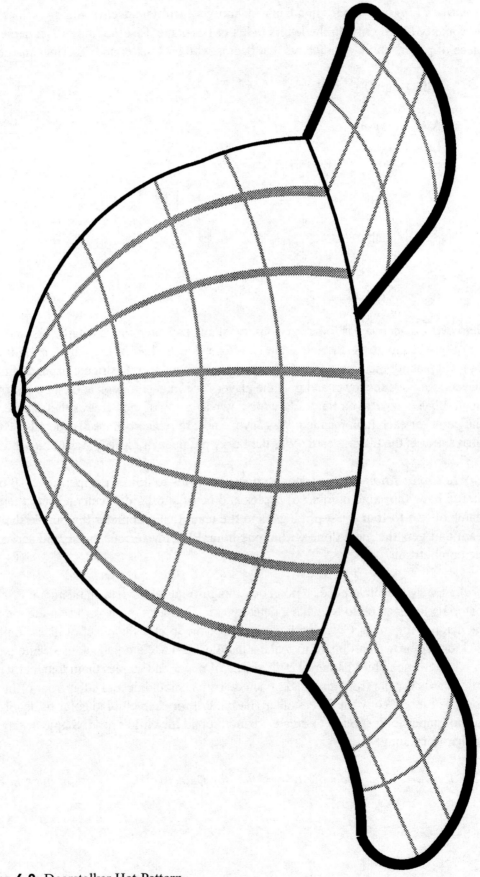

Figure 6.9: Deerstalker Hat Pattern

Mystery Story Times for Younger Children (Ages 2–6)

Story Time 1: The Case of the Missing Cookies

> **Books to Share:**
> *Case of the Backyard Treasure* by Joanne Rocklin.
> *The Eleventh Hour* by Graeme Base.
> *Tough Cookie* by David Wisniewski.
> *Who Took the Cookie from the Cookie Jar?* by Bonnie Lass.
> *Young Cam Jansen and the Missing Cookie* by David A. Adler.

Nametag—Cookie Cutter Kids: Cut girl and boy shapes (use a die-cut machine or a cookie cutter as a pattern). Let each child decorate his or her cookie person. Write the child's name on the tag.

Activity—Mouse Hunt: Read *The Eleventh Hour* and have the children try to find the mice hidden on each page. Display other books that have hidden pictures.

Activity—Food Fun: Read *Who Took the Cookie from the Cookie Jar?* and have the children participate in this action rhyme: Everyone sits in a circle. If the children do not know each other, provide nametags or simply say "you" and point the next child. Younger children can simply clap hands keeping with the rhyme, while older children can alternate slapping their thighs and clapping their hands. For more fun, substitute other foods in the rhyme. For example, "Who stole the pickle from the pickle jar?" "Who stole the mustard from the mustard jar?" See how silly you can get. Bring samples of foods to stimulate the creativity and, of course, bring cookies for the kids to eat!

Nursery Rhyme:

Who Made the Pie?
(Traditional Mother Goose)

Who made the pie?
I did.
Who stole the pie?
He did.
Who found the pie?

She did.
Who ate the pie?
You did.
Who cried for pie?
We all did!

Flannel Board—The Queen of Hearts: Prepare three hearts, each a different size, and a pie or tart to place on the flannel board as you recite the familiar nursery rhyme.

Story Time 2: Surprises

Books to Share:
Arthur's Mystery Envelope by Marc Brown.
Detective Donut and the Wild Goose Chase by Bruce Whatley.
The Mailbox Mice Mystery by Juli Mahr.
The Mud Flat Mystery by James Stevenson.

Nametag—Envelopes: Use small white envelopes as nametags. Insert a message on a piece of colored paper welcoming the child to story time or suggesting a good book to borrow.

Activity—Surprise Touch Box: A large box holds mystery for the kids in *The Mud Flat Mystery*. Touch boxes help young children develop and improve problem-solving skills. Prepare a closed box (like a shoe box or a small packing box). Cover the box with nice paper and decorate with mysterious symbols (question marks, magnifying glass, detective badges). Cut a hole in the box just large enough for a child's hand to fit through. Place small objects in the box and ask the children to guess what is in the box. Pebbles, feathers, toy cars, dog biscuits, and combs are good objects for guessers.

Food—Decorating Donuts: Use plain cake donuts, icing, sprinkles, and other goodies to let the children decorate their own donuts for eating. For a less tasty treat, give each child a donut pattern (a circle with the center cut out), glitter, crayons, lace, and rickrack and allow the kids to decorate their donuts.

Activity—Making Sense: Gather small jars, cotton balls, smelly items (vanilla extract, root beer, pickle juice, garlic, peppermint), and eye droppers. Have a piece of mesh that fits over the jar (secure with a rubber band) or punch holes in the lids. Pour or drop a small amount of one smell onto a cotton ball and put the cotton ball in the jar. Some smelly items may not need a cotton ball, but you may have to cover the jar to hide the contents (for example, peppermint candies). Prepare five or six different scents. Cover the jars securely to contain the scent (you can prepare the jars about 30 minutes ahead of time). Let each child smell the jar and guess the scent.

Film Resource: *Arthur's Mystery Files.*

Story Time 3: Cops and Robbers

Books to Share:
Crictor by Tomi Ungerer.
Emergency! by Margaret Mayo.
Georgie and the Robbers by Robert Bright.
Pet Detectives by Betty Ren Wright.
The Robbery at the Diamond Dog Diner by Eileen Christelow.

Figure 6.10: Police Paper Bag Puppet

Name Tags—Medals: Cut circles out of cardboard (or use a die-cut machine) and cover them with gold, silver, or aluminum foil. Punch a hole in the medal and attach to yarn. Use a paint pen to letter each child's name on a medal.

Puppet: Use the Police Paper Bag Puppet pattern provided to create enough police officer parts for each child. Children can color in their officer and then glue the pieces to a paper lunch sack and have a police officer puppet to take home.

Flannel Board: Use a donkey, cat, dog, and rooster flannel pieces to tell the Grimm's fairy tale "The Musicians of Bremen," a story about four friends who foil a gang of robbers.

Fingerplay—There's a Policeman:
There is a policeman (point to the
distance)
Walking on his beat (walk in place)
Another one is helping kids cross the
street (swing arm out in an offering motion)
That one blows a whistle (hold fingers to
mouth like a whistle)
And tells the traffic, STOP! (put hand up
in stopping motion)

Safety Handout: Give the children a
photocopied telephone pattern or let
them draw their own phone. Together,
practice pointing to the numbers for
9-1-1. Ask parents to help their child
write out other emergency numbers.

Figure 6.11: Police Paper Bag Illustration

Story Time 4: Mysteries of Nature

Books to Share:
The Cobweb Confession by George Edward Stanley.
Dot & Jabber and the Great Acorn Mystery by Ellen Stoll Walsh.
Dot & Jabber and the Mystery of the Missing Stream by Ellen Stoll Walsh.
What Did They See? by John Schindel.
Where do Balloons Go?: an Uplifting Mystery by Jamie Lee Curtis.

Name Tag—Balloons: Cut balloon shaped name tags or use a die-cut machine to create the shapes. Use many colors!

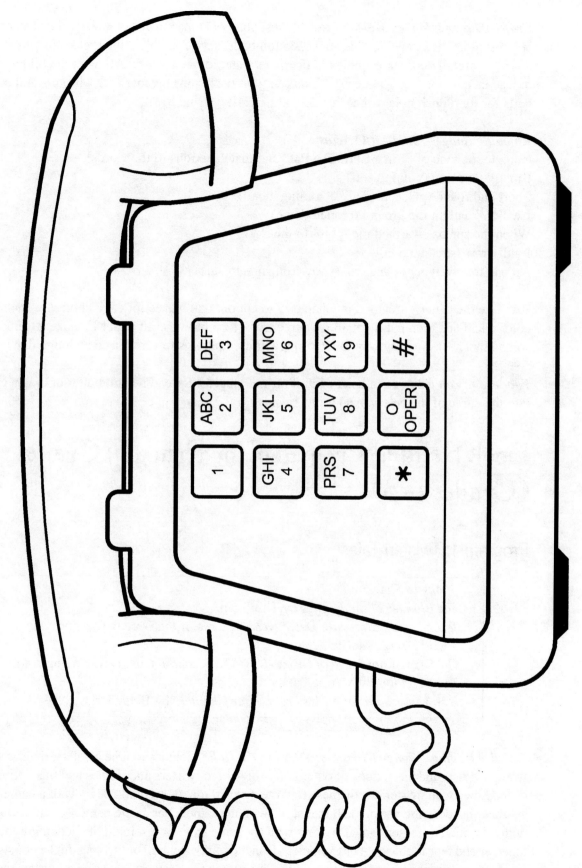

Figure 6.12: Telephone Pattern

Craft—Dot and Jabber Masks: Provide these materials: paper plates, fuzzy pipe cleaners, crayons or colored pencils, glue sticks, cotton balls, scissors, hole punch, elastic string.

Carefully cut out eyeholes in the paper plate for each mask. Allow each child to draw a mouse face on the paper plate. The kids can glue fuzzy pipe cleaners for whiskers and cotton balls for fur. Punch holes on each side and tie elastic string to fit.

Rhyming Song—I'm A Little Acorn:
(Sing to the tune of "I'm a Little Tea Pot" and match actions to the words)
I'm a little acorn (point to self)
Short and round (place hands like holding a ball)
I will fall and hit the ground (crouch down)
When the sun has warmed me (point to the sky)
I will grow (stretch up tall)
An oak tree swaying to and fro. (sway from side to side)

Art: Use the pattern provided in Chapter 5 to cut out oak leaves for each child. Let each child color a leaf and then put them all on a tree trunk (use brown craft paper to make a trunk and some branches). An easy way to let young children paint is to use non-toxic bingo daubers.

Food—Ants on a Log: Cut celery into four-inch pieces. Spread peanut butter or cream cheese into the curve of the celery. Add a few raisins for the ants.

Book Related Programs for Primary Grades (Grades 1–3)

Program 1: Twisted Tales

> **Books to Share:**
> *The Blunder of the Rogues* by Tim Egan.
> *Jake Gander, Storyville Detective: The Case of the Greedy Granny*
>   by George McClements.
> *The Secret Knowledge of Grown-Ups: The Second File* by David Wisniewski.
> *The Web Files* by Margie Patini.
> *Who's in the Hall?: a Mystery in Four Chapters* by Betsy Hearne.

Creative Writing—Tongue Twisters: Who's in the Hall? includes tongue twisters, rhymes, and wordplay. Ask students to look at other books of tongue twisters and riddles and then write some of their own with mysterious themes. To write original tongue twisters, begin with a name. Add an action (what does the person do?) that starts with the same letter as the name. Finish the twister with a location or reason that also starts with the same letter or a sound-alike letter. Put the words together and repeat quickly. For example: "Jeanette jumps gently" or "Donna dunks donuts daily." Hold a tongue twister contest. Prizes go to the children who can say the tongue twisters the most times before messing up. (Try these: "Thieves seize skis." "Good blood, bad blood.")

Creative Writing—Rewrite the Ending: Jake Gander says, "Fairy tales don't always have happy endings." It is his job to rewrite them so that they come out okay. Think about nursery rhymes and fairy tales that need happier endings and re-write them. For example, Jack and Jill should not be hurt when they fall down the hill, Humpty Dumpty could be repaired or not fall off the wall, or the big bad wolf could be rehabilitated and help the three little pigs build houses with Habitat for Humanity.

Secret Languages: Jake Gander uses codes to describe problems. For example, "P.W.T." means Possible Wolf Trouble and the story sounds suspiciously like Little Red Riding Hood. Think about other fairy tales. Decide what the problem or potential crime might be and make up a shorthand code for it. The crime in Three Billy Goats Gruff might be described as "T.L.A." for Troll Lurking About.

Twisted Character Craft: You'll need fuzzy pipe cleaners, small round magnets (available at hardware stores) or small plastic circles, and scissors to cut the pipe cleaners. Fold one pipe cleaner in half and twist through one circle to create legs. Attach another pipe cleaner for the body and twist through a magnet for the head. Twist a short pipe cleaner for arms and add smaller circles for hands and feet. Your person is now ready to bend and shape. If you used magnets, the bendable figure can be put on the refrigerator or other metal.

Art—Design a Detective: Many detectives in children's books are animals. Give each child a piece of art paper, a piece of writing paper, pencils, crayons, and other art supplies. Ask each child to choose an animal and list the characteristics of that animal that would make it a good detective. Think about places the animal could go that people cannot, things the animal might be able to find that we would miss, and physical abilities that would help the animal solve crimes. After listing these traits on the writing paper, each child should draw his or her animal detective.

Program 2: On Stage

Books to Share:
The Blue Avenger Cracks the Code by Norma Howe.
The Face in the Mirror by Stephanie Tolan.
The Ghost in the Third Row by Bruce Coville.
The Hero of Third Grade by Alice DeLaCroix.
Stage Fright on a Summer Night by Mary Pope Osborne.

Face Painting: Face painting makes a great disguise. *Face Painting* by Patricia Silver or *Face Paintings* by Chris Chaudron provides patterns, but almost anyone can do simple designs like cat faces, clowns, and villains. Be sure to purchase high quality non-toxic face paint.

Storytelling: Tell ghost stories. The Moonlit Road Web site at <http://www.themoonlitroad.com> shares some interesting examples. Are there any ghost stories from the area where you live? Ghost stories usually begin by embellishing something that really happened, so if there are no local stories, make one up.

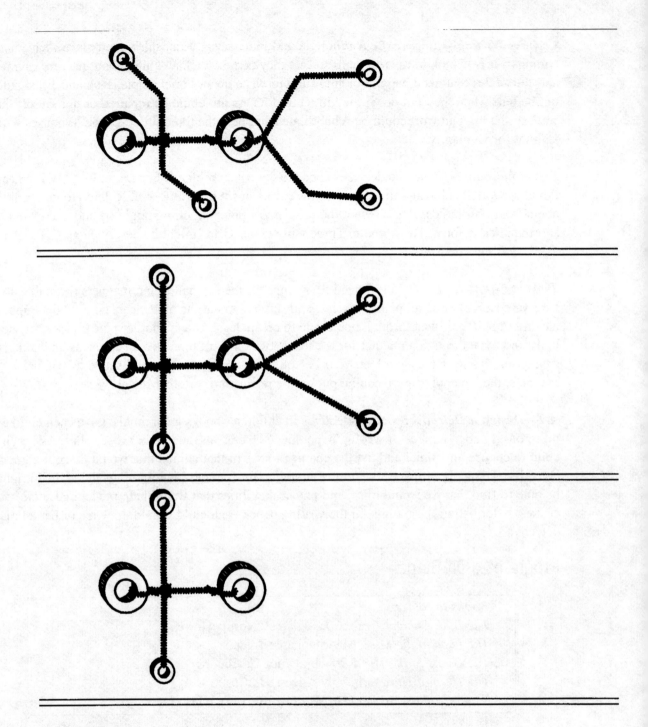

Figure 6.13: Twisted Character Illustration

Craft—Playbills: Old-style variety shows, acting troupes, and minstrels used playbills to advertise their shows and attract customers. Create playbills to promote a favorite mystery book, film, or school performance. Use large pieces of colored paper (try 17 x 22 printer paper), stencils with different font styles or rub-on lettering, colored pencils or felt tipped pens, and a ruler. Use many old-style typefaces, plenty of color, decorative rules and borders, and plenty of flamboyant language. Write out the information to be shared on a piece of scrap paper. Think about the design and layout—what will go where on the playbills? Use the ruler to create light lines. Stencil the words (or use rub-on letters), add rules and borders, color or highlight the words, and hang up your playbill. Alternately, create the playbill on the computer using clip art and computer fonts.

Program 3: The Art of Mystery

> ***Books to Share:***
> *Art Dog* by Thatcher Hurd.
> *Art Fraud Detective: Spot the Difference, Solve the Crime!* by Anna Nilsen.
> *Can You Find It?* by Judith Cressy.
> *Eggs Mark the Spot* by Mary Jane Auch.
> *The Great Googlestein Museum Mystery* by Jean Van Leeuwen.

Craft: Read *Eggs Marks the Spot* and then make art eggs. Provide plastic eggs or egg-shaped cardboard, craft glue, ribbon scraps, glitter, stickers, small "jewels," silver and gold string, small sparkly craft items, and paint pens, colored pencils, or water colors. The eggs that Pauline lays

Figure 6.14: Framed Illustration

are decorated with reproductions of paintings by Matisse, Picasso, Klee, and Van Gogh. Share pictures of the original paintings with the children. Show pictures of Faberge eggs, Ukrainian Easter eggs, and other art eggs. Children should then design their own eggs and decorate them. Use eggcups or cut sections from an egg carton to use as stands to display the art eggs.

Film Resource: Art Dog.

Guest Speaker: Invite an artist to demonstrate painting techniques and talk about how art historians decide whether a painting is really by the artist credited with the work.

Craft—Framed!: Gather old magazines with art reproductions or photographs, plastic mounts for photographic slides (they pop apart; recycle old slides by reusing the mounts or buy them new), scissors, glue sticks, and pin backs. Allow the children to find a photograph or an art reproduction that suits their interests. Cut the photograph to be a little larger than the opening of the slide mount. Glue in place. Glue a pin back onto the back of the mount. For a more ornate pin, add sparkles, small jewels, or other decoration to the frame. For larger projects, use cardboard frames designed for transparencies. Decorate the frame and then glue the photograph or art reproduction in place and display.

Activity—Art Dog Masks: Use the template to create a blank mask for each child. Display art by a variety of artists, including Picasso, Klee, Monet, and Van Gogh. Provide art supplies and let each child create an art dog in the style of a famous painter.

Programs for Intermediate Grades (Grades 4–6)

Program 1: Police Work

Books to Share:
Aero and Officer Mike: Police Partners by Joan Plummer Russell.
Case Closed: The Real Scoop on Detective Work by Milton Meltzer.
Chase by Alison Hart.
Rescue by Alison Hart.
The Treasure of Bessledorf Hill by Phyllis Reynolds Naylor.

Creative Writing: Written with the cooperation and assistance of the Staunton, Virginia, Police Department, *Chase and Rescue* by Alison Hart focus on fictional crimes in a realistic manner. The cases are inspired by true events and the names of real police officers are used as readers experience the language, techniques, and equipment used by police every day. Photographs and minute-by-minute details add to the realism. Use the local newspaper to find recent police cases. Write a fictional story, incorporating names and events, about the case. Add photographs and details.

Guest Speaker: Invite a police officer to speak to the group. Ask the officer to explain the special equipment used in law enforcement. Ask about new specialties in law enforcement. For

Figure 6.15: Dog Mask Pattern

example, technology has created jobs for people who can use computer files and the Internet to track criminals.

Art: Use the pattern provided to have students design a badge for their own police department.

Research: Use *Careers for Mystery Buffs and Other Snoops and Sleuths* by Blythe Camenson or other career encyclopedias to explore other professions that work to solve crimes. Each child should then draw a picture of himself or herself working in that career, write a short description of the career, or find information about a famous person who worked in the field.

Program 2: Family Problems

Books to Share:
Alias by Elizabeth Ryan.
Disappearing Act by Sid Fleischman.
Finding Zola by Marianne Mitchell.
How to Disappear Completely and Never Be Found by Sara Nickerson.
Son of the Mob by Gordon Korman.

Writing Activity—Screenplay: Read the introductory paragraph in *How to Disappear Completely and Never Be Found*. Nickerson first wrote the book as a screenplay. Ask the students to re-write a chapter as a screenplay, including dialogue, action, and so on. *Writing Mysteries, Movies, Monster Stories, and More* by Nancy Bentley and Donna Guthrie provides guidance on developing a screenplay. A screenplay generally has three acts: the setup, the confrontation, and the resolution. Select a couple of plot points. Have the students write up the scene and dialogue. Act out the scene. Add costumes and film the scene with a digital video camera.

Discussion: Discuss the reasons someone might have for disappearing. How easy or difficult would it be to do? What resources would someone need? List items that most people must have to get by in their daily lives (identification, money, a job).

Scavenger Hunt: Nickerson says, "I thought wouldn't it be great if a character left clues to a small-town mystery by slipping handwritten books into the local library?" Arrange a scavenger hunt leading the participants to specific books to find clues. This should be an opportunity for the kids to examine a variety of different kinds of library materials.

Craft—Missing Persons: A lot of jigsaw puzzle pieces look a bit like people. Recycle old jigsaw puzzles that are missing some pieces to create "missing person" pins. Kids can decorate the pieces with poster paint or use glue to attach a small photograph of a face and pieces of paper for clothing. Glue a pin back (available at craft supply stores) to the back of the puzzle piece. Let it dry and it is ready to wear!

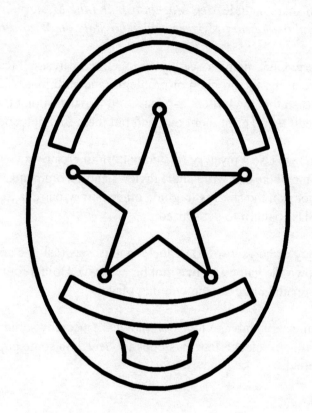

Figure 6.16: Police Badge Pattern

Program 3: Mystery Club

Set up a desk to serve as the office for the Library Detection Agency. Look at movie stills from detective films and try to make your agency look similar. Borrow an old-fashioned typewriter and a desk lamp. A fedora hat, a trench coat, and stacks of manila folders will add to the ambiance.

Send invitations to join the Mystery Club. They can be shaped like a magnifying glass giving the day and time the club will meet. Alternatively, give some of the details in secret code and offer a small prize at the first meeting to those who solved the code.

Read mysteries set in a library or booktalk them. Discuss what it would be like to be locked in the library. If you are brave, hold an after-hours party for the Mystery Club members. Some books to share include *Meg Mackintosh and the Mystery in the Locked Library, Young Cam Jansen and the Library Mystery*, and *Who Stole the Wizard of Oz?*

Write a Mystery: Club members can work together or in small teams to write a mystery. Decide on characters, setting, the problem or problems, and solutions. Add clues and brainstorm a variety of solutions so that the writers can leave red herrings along the way. After the mysteries have been written, edit them, print them out, and put them in a notebook for all to enjoy.

Shelf Suggestions: Use a mystery related pattern to create "review cards" for the bookshelves. Mystery club members can write short reviews and recommendations for mysteries. Place the recommendations on the shelves to guide other library patrons to suggested readings. Use the Magnifying Glass pattern to get started.

Get a Clue: Buy or borrow several Clue™ games sets (ask the community for donations as many people own the game and may not be using it). Hold a round robin Clue™ competition. Give mystery related prizes to the winning players.

Film Fest: A mystery club can focus on movies, especially some of the really bad or silly ones. Ask the kids to help select a few mysteries to view. Pop some popcorn, make some mystery punch, and enjoy!

Mysteries for Young Adults

Booktalk: Paper Trail by Barbara Snow Gilbert. A 15-year-old boy peers out of the hollow tree in which he is hiding. He hears his mother calling his name. He is startled—his mother was supposed to be running away, acting as a decoy to lead the pursuers away from him and his father! His father was supposed to circle around and make sure the woods were clear. Only then would he be able to escape the "patriotic" group that called themselves the Soldiers of God. Instead of assurances that all is okay, the boy hears the crack of a sniper's rifle and watches in horror as his mother is shot. Intermingled with the boy's story are snippets from real news reports, government documents, and books about paramilitary hate groups. This is a story of survival, deception, and secret lives that keeps you guessing until the very end.

Activity One—Maps and Orienteering: Orienteering is a sport in which competitors follow a course with a map and a compass. Usually the courses are set in forests and wooded areas, but

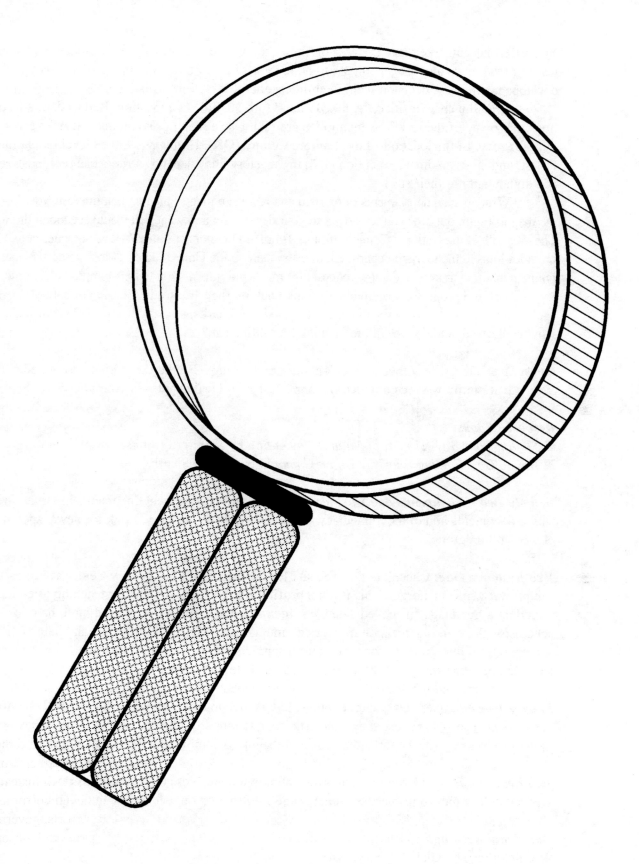

Figure 6.17: Magnifying Glass Pattern

smaller events can take place in parks or almost anywhere that provides a challenge. Participants learn to read maps and use a compass to hone their sense of direction. Orienteering uses and develops math skills, decision-making abilities, and observation skills.

Read the chapter titled, "A Fixed Point" (pp. 30–36). The location, Red Cedar, is fictitious, but many of the locations mentioned are real. Use a map of Oklahoma and Arkansas to look for some of the locations. Find LaFlore County (OK), Highway 59, the Ouachita National Forest, and other landmarks mentioned. Many mystery and suspense writers use real locations to add authenticity to their stories.

Write to state departments of tourism and request a map of an area that interests you. Use the map to figure out how you would get to your destination and what you would see along the way. The Web site of the National Council of State Tourism Directors at <http://www.tourstates.com/> provides links to the tourism department of every state in the United States. (Most states also have an online map on their sites and allow requests for maps and information to be submitted electronically.)

Ask the program participants to think back on their trip to the library (or school). Ask each student to write down the distances traveled, landmarks, and any unusual observations. How well could students recall the details of a routine trip?

Guest Speaker: Invite someone to talk about orienteering. Use the U.S. Orienteering Federation Web site at <http://www.us.orienteering.org/> to find a local chapter in your area.

Resource Books:
■ *Finding Your Way: The Art of Natural Navigation* by Jennifer Owings Dewey.
■ *Way to Go!: Finding Your Way with a Compass* by Sharon Sharth.

Activity Two—Documents and Further Research: Gilbert cites real documents in *Paper Trail*. These documents add to the immediacy and authenticity of the story. Look for newspaper articles on militia groups.

Web Resource One: Check out the Web site for the Southern Poverty Law Center at <http://www.splcenter.org/>. This is a nonprofit group that offers ideas for teaching tolerance, including a free magazine called *Teaching Tolerance* and a guide for responding to hate in schools. Is there an organization in your community that combats intolerance and hate? Ask someone from that group to speak to your group. Discuss why people are sometimes intolerant and what happens when that intolerance becomes hate that leads to violence.

Nothing But the Truth by Avi is told entirely using documents. Kate Klise's book *Trial by Jury Journal* mixes newspaperclippings, letters, documents, and other items to tell the story. Let students use newspapers, magazine articles, citations from books, or memos that they develop themselves to write a short story. Use a notebook to compile the items that support the story.

Web Resource Two: The National Archives <http://www.archives.gov/digital_classroom/> provide reproducible copies of primary documents and information on teaching with documents.

Additional Reading:
■ *Camouflage* by Gloria D. Miklowitz.
■ *Dead Girls Don't Write Letters* by Gail Giles.
■ *Flight of the Raven* by Stephanie Tolan.
■ *Lemony Snicket: The Unauthorized Autobiography* by Lemony Snicket.

Read Aloud: *Who Are You?* by Joan Lowery Nixon. Read aloud from page 53 to page 57, ending with the sentence " 'Some forgers are so talented that it's very hard for even the experts to tell the copies from the real thing,' Ms. Montero explains." This passage describes how art is stolen from museums or replaced by forgeries.

Look up articles about the 1911 theft of the Mona Lisa. Display samples of great works of art and let the students make their own "copies."

Web Search: Use the Lycoskids Info Please Web site at <http://kids.infoplease.lycos.com> to find information on art forgeries. (Enter the phrase "forgery, in art.") Encarta at <http://encarta.msn.com> also has an article on art forgeries that includes information on the scientific processes used to detect forgeries. Search Art News Online at <http://www.artnewsonline.com> for articles on forgery, including "The So-Called Van Goghs."

Discussion One: What does the word "provenance" mean? Vincent van Gogh's "Garden at Auvers" was declared a forgery because the provenance was incomplete. Ask the students to think about something they have that is very old, such as a family heirloom or an item that belonged to a grandparent. What do they know about the history of the item? What can they find out through research and interviews?

Discussion Two: Is forgery different from counterfeiting? What items other than art do criminals forge? Invite a banker to discuss the ways counterfeit money is detected.

Activity: Use *Art Fraud Detective* by Anna Nilsen to start a discussion about art. Students should pick one artist and do additional research. What other paintings did the artist create? What museums own the artist's work? Check the Internet and newspaper or periodical indices to find out if any of the artist's paintings have ever been stolen or forged. Search online auction houses to see if any paintings are being offered for sale or what recent sales have been.

Related Titles:
- *From the Mixed-Up Files of Mrs. Basil E. Frankweiler* by E.L. Konigsberg.
- *The Sylvia Game* by Vivien Alcock.
- *Who Stole the Wizard of Oz?* by Avi.

Booktalk: *The Body of Christopher Creed* by Carol Plum-Ucci. The hardest crimes to deal with are the ones that have no resolution. When Christopher Creed disappears without a trace, 16-year-old Torey Adams faces a traumatic point in his life. Chris had been the class freak, bullied by most of the other kids, but the true weirdness of his life comes out after he disappears. Looking back at what happened, Torey becomes obsessed with learning what happened to Chris Creed. The only clue is a cryptic e-mail message. The story unfolds through Torey's memoir about the events from his past and his reflections on how the kids in his small town stereotyped and isolated Chris. However, did two of the town's kids murder Chris, or did he simply walk away to a new life? Some mysteries are never solved.

Discussion: A group of kids is referred to as "the boons" because the kids live in an area called "the boondocks." Talk about cliques. What are the popular kids called? Are there labels that hurt or demean less popular kids? Most mystery stories have a "happy ending." Good triumphs over evil; the criminal is punished; justice prevails. That does not always happen in real life.

Creative Writing: Chris kept a journal that contained many embellishments, dreams, and half-truths. Talk about journal writing and allow each student to make a journal; if funds permit, purchase small plain journal books, and have each child decorate his or her journal with markers, stickers, and so on.

Discussion: Torey posted his memoir to the Internet and received replies from people who believe that Creed is still alive. Talk about why we often cling to the hope that someone is still alive. Look at the stories of others who have disappeared without a trace (Aimee Semple McPherson, Amelia Earhart).

Related Books:
■ *Counterfeit Son* by Elaine Marie Aphin.
■ *I Dream of Murder* by Catherine Dexter.
■ *Martyn Pig* by Kevin Brooks.
■ *When Dad Killed Mom* by Julius Lester.

Graphic Novels

For reluctant readers, boys who are "too cool" for reading, or children who will not leave the computers, graphic novels can serve as a bridge to reading. Graphic novels are available in all genres, so kids who rarely read anything else may pick up a mystery graphic novel. Librarians and teachers can then help those students transition to other reading material.

Many graphic novels are well written and have sophisticated vocabulary and complicated plots. The graphics portray the actions and allow the reader to see the setting and facial expressions in place of textual descriptions. Do keep in mind that not every graphic novel is for every reader; the illustrations can be a bit racy and graphic (no pun intended). At the other end of the range are the Scooby Doo mysteries, which are tame by any standards and could satisfy demand for graphic novels from young children. Check reviews and talk to the sales staff at your local comic book store—they are usually happy to help even if you cannot make library purchases there.

For an extensive bibliography and information on selecting and programming with graphic novels, consult *Getting Graphic! Using Graphic Novels to Promote Literacy With Teens* by Michele Gorman, published by Linworth Publishing.

Related Books:
Batman: The Long Halloween by Jeph Loeb and Tim Sale. Batman receives more tricks than treats when a series of holiday murders and a crime spree leave him longing for the night to end.

The Borden Tragedy: A Memoir of the Infamous Double Murder at Fall River, Mass, 1892 by Rick Geary. Readers view the scene of the crime and observe the investigation from several angles in the presentation of this unsolved historic mystery.

The Crimebusters Investigate by Mark Fowler. Kaz Smiley and her friend, Mat, investigate a jewel heist and try to thwart a criminal mastermind who is threatening the old city of Allegro.

Powers: Who Killed Retro Girl? by Brian Michael Bendis. Homicide detective, Christian Walker, investigates the murder of one of the world's most beloved superheroes, Retro Girl.

Raymond Chandler's Philip Marlowe: The Little Sister by Raymond Chandler and Michael Lark. Full-color illustrations capture Marlowe's Los Angeles and bring this class novel to life.

Steam Detectives by Kia Asamiya. A fictional character goes on a murder spree, but his creator will be blamed for the crime unless detective Narutaki can find the real killer.

Appendixes

"Has anything escaped me? I trust there is nothing of consequence which I have overlooked?" —Dr. Watson, *Hound of the Baskervilles*

Awards for Mystery Literature

Edgar Allan Poe Award

The Edgar Awards are given annually by the Mystery Writers of America, the professional association for mystery writers. In addition to several categories for adult books, nonfiction, short stories, and movie and television scripts, an award is given for the best juvenile book and the best young adult book. Until 1989, young adult and children's books were judged together, so some early titles may not be appropriate for elementary school-aged children. Both nominees and winners are usually good selections, especially for libraries and classroom collections with limited budgets for purchasing new titles.

Winners since 1994 are listed, but all past winners, nominees, and future awards can be found on the Mystery Writers of America Web site at <http://www.mysterywriters.org>, which includes a searchable database of all nominees and winners.

Best Juvenile Mystery

2003: *Harriet Spies Again* by Helen Ericson.
2002: *Dangling* by Lillian Eige.
2001: *Dovey Coe* by Frances O'Roark Dowell.
2000: *The Night Flyers* by Elizabeth McDavid Jones.
1999: *Sammy Keyes and the Hotel Thief* by Wendelin Van Draanen.
1998: *Sparrows in the Scullery* by Barbara Brooks Wallace.
1997: *The Clearing* by Dorothy Reynolds Miller.
1996: *Looking for Jamie Bridger* by Nancy Springer.
1995: *The Absolutely True Story ... How I Visited Yellowstone Park with the Terrible Rubes* by Willo Davis Roberts.
1994: *The Twin in the Tavern* by Barbara Brooks Wallace.

Best Young Adult Mystery

2003: *The Wessex Papers, Vols. 1–3* by Daniel Parker.
2002: *The Boy in the Burning House* by Tim Wynne-Jones.

2001: *Counterfeit Son* by Elaine Marie Alphin.
2000: *Never Trust a Dead Man* by Vivian Vande Velde.
1999: *The Killer's Cousin* by Nancy Werlin.
1998: *Ghost Canoe* by Will Hobbs.
1997: *Twisted Summer* by Willo Davis Roberts.
1996: *Prophecy Rock* by Rob MacGregor.
1995: *Toughing It* by Nancy Springer.
1994: *The Name of the Game Was Murder* by Joan Lowery Nixon.

Arthur Ellis Award

Similar to the Edgar, the Crime Writers of Canada give an annual award to the best juvenile novel for mysteries written by Canadian authors or authors living in Canada. For more information and winners, visit the Web site at <http://www.crimewriterscanada.com/>.

2003: *Break and Enter* by Norah McClintock.
2002: *Scared to Death* by Norah McClintock.
2001: *The Boy in the Burning House* by Tim Wynne-Jones.
2000: *How Can a Brilliant Detective Shine in the Dark?* Linda Bailey.
1999: *Sins of the Father* by Norah McClintock.
1998: *The Body in the Basement* by Norah McClintock.

Local Contest

Many mystery awards are named for writers and the recipient receives a statute of the person (the Edgar) or something that symbolizes that person's work (a teapot for the Agatha). Develop your own local award for a favorite mystery selected by children in your school or public library. What will the award be called? What criteria will be used to select the winner?

Commercial Resources

These commercial enterprises sell items related to mysteries, mystery plays, and crime.

Femmes Fatales <http://www.mysterygifts.biz>
800-596-DEAD
Offers gifts for mystery fans and writers. Available items include mystery stickers, whimsical-magnets, evidence and crime scene tape, pins, T-shirts, and more.

Oriental Trading Company <http://www.orientaltrading.com>
800-228-2269
Sells carnival prizes and decorations, including police and pirate hats, badges and handcuffs, false mustaches, magnifying glasses, and more.

Mindware: Creative Enrichment for School Age Kids <http://www.mindwareonline.com/>
800-999-0398
Offers a variety of mystery related games, party plans, and puzzles.

Double Dog Press Mystery Games <http://www.hpress.highsmith.com/>
Interactive mystery games and plays developed especially for libraries.

Whodunnit Mystery Games <http://www.whodunnitmysteries.com>
877-400-0995
Interactive games for various sized groups.

Commercial sources for professional investigative materials sell to the public and educational organizations. Crime scene tape, fingerprinting cards and ink, crime scene templates, and other supplies are available from companies like Evident <http://www.evidentcrimescene.com> and Chief Supply <http://www.chiefsupply.com>. These companies won't sell badges and other items that could identify a person as a law enforcement official. Be forewarned that, since these companies primarily serve law enforcement agencies, morbid supplies—like body bags—are also available. Even the Los Angeles County coroner <http://coroner.co.la.ca.us/gifts> has a gift shop where you can purchase body shaped post-it pads, mini-badges, and T-shirts.

Online Resources

These online resources offer general information or resources that will complement many mystery-related classroom activities. Additionally, most publishers and many authors maintain Web sites that include information on their books. Be sure to confirm that the Web site address is still accurate and that the information provided is still relevant and appropriate.

TheCase.com for Kids: Fun and Challenging Mysteries for Kids at <http://www.TheCase.com/kids> offers mini-mysteries, scary stories, magic tricks, and contests that change regularly. A free online club allows children to receive a new mystery via e-mail weekly. "Learning with Mysteries" provides suggestions for educators to use mysteries to teach critical thinking and deductive reasoning.

The Crime Library at <http://www.crimelibrary.com/> provides information about hundreds of notorious crimes and biographies of famous criminals and crime fighters, along with informational articles on the criminal mind, profiling, forensics, and more (note that some pages contain graphic language and photos, but the site is extremely extensive and useful for research).

Crime Scene Evidence Files at <http://www.kudzukids.com> is part of a "true crime" Web site. It is set in the fictional county of Yoknapatawpha, Mississippi. More suitable for high-school students and adults, it also has an investigation for younger children to solve.

The FBI's Web site at <http://www.fbi.gov/fbikids.htm> offers information for kids, divided into two groups (K–5; 6–12). Learn how dogs are used in investigations, follow a case through the FBI lab, learn about a typical day for an agent, view a time line of cases, and play games.

The Freedom of Information Act at <http://foia.fbi.gov> allows the public access to government files. Many FBI files related to criminal investigations are available (click on electronic reading room for a list of files available).

Kids Read at <http://www.kidsreads.com> provides an assortment of resources related to books and authors. The site provides word search and trivia games for many mysteries, including the Lemony Snicket series, Encyclopedia Brown, and A to Z Mysteries.

Law for Kids at <http://www.lawforkids.org> is a project of the Arizona Foundation for Legal Services and Education. The site offers information about legal rights, copies of important legal documents, animated cartoons about children learning the law, and answers to questions about Arizona law (a companion Web site offers the same information in Spanish).

Library of Congress American Memory Web site at <http://memory.loc.gov/ammem/ndlpedu> has links to documents, photographs, and other information related to a wide variety of topics including crime, laws, legislation, legislators, and violence. Many primary documents are available in electronic format. Use the Today in History archives at <http://lcweb2.loc.gov/ammem/today/archive.html> to find historic events that tie in with lesson plans or activities.

Mystery Net at <http://www.mysterynet.com> offers information, mystery games, profiles of great writers, and a time line. On a sub-page <http://kids.mysterynet.com/>, there are mysteries for kids.

The Poe Museum at <http://www.poemuseum.org> provides details about Edgar Allan Poe's life and the mystery surrounding his death, as well as sample lesson plans for teaching Poe and links to online versions of his stories.

Sherlock Holmes on the Web at <http://www.sherlockian.net> provides everything anyone might ever want to know about the great detective. Links to the stories, chronologies, frequently asked questions, film and television versions, and more will answer almost any question.

Annotated List of Film/Video Resources

Use video or DVD films for mystery programs or to supplement classroom activities. Mystery movies are also popular selections for library checkout for home use.

The Apple Dumpling Gang. Disney, 1997. 100 mins. Don Knotts and Tim Conway are outlaws who meet up with a gang of kids with hilarious results. Grades 3–7.

Art Dog. Live Oak, 1996. 8 mins. Art Dog is a guard at the art museum and he becomes a suspect when one of the paintings is stolen. Preschool–Grade 2.

Arthur's Mystery Files. WGBH, 2001. 40 mins. This video includes three Arthur mysteries— *Arthur Accused, Fern's Slumber Party,* and *Binky Rules.* Preschool–Grade 2.

The Bugs Bunny Mystery Special. Warner Home Video, 1993. 24 mins. Bugs Bunny and Elmer Fudd introduce clips from a variety of classic "crime" cartoons in a tribute to Alfred Hitchcock. Originally released for television in 1980. Grades 3–8.

Dog Day's of the West. Lyrick Studios, 1998. 92 mins. Wishbone goes to the Old West to save a dusty town from a dastardly bad guy in this O. Henry short story. Grades 3–6.

The Dollhouse Murders. AIMS, 1993. 62 mins. Twelve-year-old Amy discovers a dollhouse and becomes frightened when mysterious events begin to occur. Grades 3–7.

Encyclopedia Brown, the Boy Detective, in The Case of the Amazing Race Car. Sony, 1999. 26 mins. Based upon the stories by Donald J. Sobol. Encyclopedia Brown investigates the case of the missing go-cart. He has three clues, but will he find the missing car in time for the championship? Grades 2–6.

From the Mixed-Up Files of Mrs. Basil E. Frankweiler. Phoenix Films, 1976. 30 mins. Claudia and her brother search out the mysterious origins of a sculpture they see in the Metropolitan Museum of Art. Could it really be the work of Michelangelo? The clues lead them to Mrs. Frankeweiler, portrayed by Ingrid Bergman. Grades 3–7.

The Great Mouse Detective. Buena Vista, 1986. 74 mins. Mouse super-sleuth, Basil, and his sidekick, Dawson, outwit the ruthless Professor Ratigan in this animated film based on Eve Titus's classic mystery, *Basil of Baker Street.* Grades 2–7.

The Gold Bug. Phoenix Films, 1980. 31 mins. This ABC Weekend Special production of Poe's classic story tells of a young boy who finds an old piece of paper with a secret code.

Harriet the Spy. Paramount, 1996. 102 mins. Rosie O'Donnell stars in this feature-length film about a young girl and her secret notebook. Grades 3–7.

It's a Mystery, Charlie Brown. Paramount, 1987. 30 mins. When someone steals Woodstock's nest, detective Snoopy, dressed as Sherlock Holmes, is on the case. Grades 2–6.

Little Bear: Campfire Tales. Paramount, 2002. 35 mins. Based on the books by Else Holmelund Minarik and Maurice Sendak, Little Bear and friends have four adventures when they set up camp in the backyard. Preschool–Grade 2.

Murder She Purred: A Mrs. Murphy Mystery. Disney, 1998. Based on the novels of Rita Mae Brown, cat and dog sleuths dig up the dirt in a small town and solve a murder. Grade 4–Adult.

In Search of History: Pirates of the Barbary Coast. A&E Home Video, 1998. 50 mins. This production examines the pirates in 18th century America and the creation of the U.S. Navy. Grade 4–Adult.

The Real McCaw. Paramount, 1997. 92 mins. Sam finds out about a century-old pirate's treasure chest from Mac, a 150-year-old talking parrot. The 13-year-old boy and the parrot set out to find the buried treasure and help Sam's grandfather stay out of bankruptcy. Grades 4–8.

Sherlock Holmes, the Great Detective. A&E Home Video, 1995. 50 mins. A&E's "Biography" series explores Sherlock Holmes and Sir Arthur Conan Doyle, examining Holmes' cases and logical deductions. Grade 6–Adult.

Spy Kids. Buena Vista, 2001. 88 mins. When their spy-team parents are kidnapped, the Cortez kids set out on their first mission to find the culprit and rescue their parents. Grades 4–8.

Annotated Bibliography of Professional Resources

These books offer additional mystery related resources for teachers and librarians looking for more ideas to use in planning programs and curricula.

Conklin, Tom. *Mystery Plays: 8 Plays for the Classroom.* New York: Scholastic, 1997. 77 p. This collection of eight plays based on detective stories by famous mystery authors offers choices for classroom productions.

Erlenbusch, Sue Jones. *Tales of Mystery, Suspense, and the Supernatural.* New York: Simon & Schuster, 1995. 358 p. Ready-to-use quizzes, projects, and activities supplement classroom activities for students in grades 4–8.

See, Betty M. *Jury Trials in the Classroom.* Westport, CT: Libraries Unlimited, 1998. 163 p. Teachers can involve students in grades 5–8 in the judicial process by staging simulated trials. The author includes three criminal trials and three civil trials featuring characters from literature and history.

Walker, Pam. *Crime Scene Investigations: Real-Life Science Activities for the Elementary Grades.* Hoboken, NJ: Jossey-Bass, 1999. 272 p. Classroom activities explore scientific investigation methods for solving crimes.

Wiese, Jim. *Detective Science: 40 Crime-Solving, Case-Breaking, Crook-Catching Activities for Kids.* Hoboken, NJ: John Wiley & Sons, 1996. 128 p. Budding detectives are invited to search for clues, gather evidence, and experience detective work first-hand.

Annotated List of Reference Resources

These books are most useful for student or teacher research. Because they are multi-volume and comprehensive on the subject, they will usually be found in high-school or public library reference collections.

Brannen, Daniel E. *Supreme Court Drama: Cases that Changed the Nation.* Detroit: UXL, 2000. 800 p. Four-volume illustrated set provides details about 150 major cases that had an impact on our nation. Grades 6–10.

Frost-Knappman, Elizabeth. *Courtroom Drama: 120 of the World's Most Notable Trials.* Detroit: UXL, Publisher, 1997. 864 p. Three-volume illustrated set provides details about U.S. and international trials from Socrates to the Supreme Court. Grades 6–12.

Levinson, David, ed. *The Encyclopedia of Crime and Punishment.* Thousand Oaks, CA: Sage Reference, 2002. 2104 p. Four-volume encyclopedia offers more than 400 articles, primary source documents, and illustrations on all facets of criminal justice. High School–Adult.

MacNee, Marie J. *Outlaws, Mobsters and Crooks: From the Old West to the Internet.* Detroit: UXL, 1998. 495 p. Three-volume illustrated set examines organized crime by category of criminal and explores the lives of 75 criminals from pirates to computer hackers. Grades 6–10.

Sifakis, Carl. *Mafia Encyclopedia.* New York: Facts on File, 1987. 367 p. An A–Z compendium of information about organized crime figures, the Mafia, and its activities and crimes. High School–Adult.

Celebrating Mysteries

Use these literary celebrations, mystery author birthdays, and memorable dates related to mysteries to focus on mystery books. Plan a party, schedule a program, design a bulletin board, or read a few chapters from a mystery.

January 19—Edgar Allan Poe's Birthday
January 7—Sherlock Holmes' Birthday
February 3—Joan Lowery Nixon's Birthday
March 13—Ellen Raskin's Birthday
May 22—Sir Arthur Conan Doyle's Birthday
August 13—Alfred Hitchcock's Birthday
September 15—Agatha Christie's Birthday
October—Kids Love a Mystery Week
October—Crime Prevention Month
October 4—Donald Sobol's Birthday
November—Child Safety and Protection Month
November 12—Marjorie Weinman Sharmat's Birthday

Bibliography

Each of the titles in this bibliography is mentioned in the text. Generally, only one or two titles for a series are included, but teachers and librarians may want to consider other titles based on popularity. Suggested grade levels are provided for each book and, unless noted, all of the books were available for purchase at the time of writing. Books mentioned in the text that are not directly related to mysteries are not included in the Bibliography.

Aaseng, Nathan. *The O.J. Simpson Trial: What it Shows us About Our Legal System.* New York: Walker, 1996. 124 p. The trial of O.J. Simpson provides the backdrop for a discussion of the criminal justice system. Grades 6–9.

Adler, David A. *Andy Russell NOT Wanted by the Police.* New York: Gulliver, 2001. 118 p. The fifth book in this series finds the young detective calling the police to help investigate suspicious activities at a neighbor's house. Grades 3–6.

_____. *Cam Jansen and the Birthday Mystery.* New York: Puffin, 2002. 64 p. Cam's surprise birthday party for her parents almost turns to disaster when her grandparents have their luggage stolen. Fortunately, Cam's photographic memory provides the critical clue. Grades 2–4.

_____. *Cam Jansen and the Mystery of the Stolen Diamonds.* New York: Puffin, 1997. 64 p. Cam uses her detection skills to find a jewel thief. Grades 2–4.

_____. *Young Cam Jansen and the Library Mystery.* New York: Puffin, 2002. 32 p. When Cam and her father visit the library to find a mystery to read, Cam uses her skills to solve a real mystery. Grades K–2.

_____. *Young Cam Jansen and the Missing Cookie.* New York: Viking, 1996. 32 p. When a classmate's cookie is missing at lunch, young Cam uses her photographic memory to discover what happened. Grades 1–2.

Ahlberg, Janet and Allan Ahlberg. *Each Peach Pear Plum.* New York: Viking, 1979. 32 p. Nursery rhymes encourage young readers to "spy" the characters hidden in the art. Preschool.

Aiken, Joan. *Wolves of Willoughby Chase.* New York: Delacorte, 2000. 160 p. Left in the care of a cruel guardian, Sylvia and Bonnie are sent to an orphan's home. Can they reclaim Willoughby Chase from evil Miss Slighcarp? Grades 5–7.

Alcock, Vivien. *The Sylvia Game.* Boston, MA: Houghton Mifflin, 1997. 216 p. While tailing her artist father, Sylvia gets mixed up in a game that leads to danger. Grades 4–6.

Aliki. *Mummies Made in Egypt.* New York: Harper, 1985. 32 p. In her typical fashion, Aliki clearly describes the mummification process and the beliefs related to Egyptian afterlife. Grades K–3.

Alphin, Elaine Marie. *Counterfeit Son.* San Diego, CA: Harcourt, 2000. 180 p. When the man he thinks is his father is killed by the police, 14-year-old Cameron uses the opportunity to assume a fake identity as the kidnapped son of another family. Grades 6–8.

Anastasio, Dina. *The Case of the Grand Canyon Eagle.* Lanham, MI: Roberts Rinehart, 1994. 96 p. While on vacation, veterinary student Juliet Stone discovers a distraught eagle and investigates the disappearance of the eagle's eggs. Grades 7–9.

Andryszewski, Tricia. *The Amazing Life of Moe Berg: Catcher, Scholar, Spy.* Brookfield, CT: Millbrook, 1996. 128 p. Princeton graduate, major league baseball player, spy for the U.S. government—the biography of Morris Berg reads like fiction, but it is fact. Grades 6–9.

Arthur, Robert. *Mystery of the Whispering Mummy.* New York: Random, 1985. 180 p. A 3000-year-old mummy leads the three investigators on a search for a curse. Grades 4–6.

Auch, Mary Jane. *Eggs Mark the Spot.* New York: Holiday House, 1996. 32 p. Pauline saves the day when her talent for laying artistic eggs helps to catch an art thief. Preschool–2.
_____. *I Was a Third Grade Spy.* New York: Holiday House, 2001. 86 p. Brian's dog, Arful, was hypnotized during the experiment in *I Was a Third Grade Science Project* and can now speak. The boys keep this talent a secret so Arful can spy on Emily Venable. Grades 2–4.

Avi. *The Man Who Was Poe.* New York: Camelot, 1997. 128 p. A boy has to find his missing family and gets some help from a mysterious stranger. Grades 3–6.
_____. *Nothing But the Truth.* New York: Flare, 1993. 224 p. Suspended for humming the national anthem, Philip believes that he has been denied his legal rights. Memos, documents, and clippings help him to prove his case. Grades 6–10.
_____. *Something Upstairs: a Tale of Ghosts.* New York: Orchard, 1999. 116 p. The ghost of a murdered slave pulls a young boy back in time to solve the crime. Grades 4–6.
_____. *Who Stole the Wizard of Oz?* New York: Random, 1990. 116 p. Becky tries to clear her name after she is accused of stealing a rare book from the local library. Grades 3–5.
_____. *Wolf Rider.* New York: Simon & Schuster, 1986. 216 p. Andy finds his own life is in danger after he mistakenly receives a call from a stranger who confesses that he has murdered someone. Grades 4–7.

Bailey, Linda. *How Can a Brilliant Detective Shine in the Dark?* Tonawanda, NY: Kids Can Press, 2003. 198 p. Stevie Diamond attends a family reunion and discovers a mystery in her own backyard and figures out why her uncle ran away 45 years earlier. Grades 3–6.
_____. *What's a Serious Detective Like Me Doing in Such a Silly Movie?* Tonawanda, NY: Kids Can Press, 2003. 189 p. Stevie Diamond jumps at the chance to be in a movie but finds herself in the middle of a mystery. Grades 4–6.

Banks, Kate. *Howie Bowles, Secret Agent.* New York: Farrar, 1999. 89 p. When Howie moves to a new town, he tries to make his new third-grade classmates believe that he is a secret agent. Grades 3–4.

Base, Graeme. *The Eleventh Hour.* New York: Harry N. Abrams, 1989. 32 p. A mystery in verse offers young readers a real challenge as they try to figure out who stole the birthday feast. Preschool–3.

Bellairs, John. *The House With A Clock In Its Walls*. New York: Yearling, 1993. 179 p. Lewis discovers secret passages, hidden rooms, and other mysteries that lead to chilling adventures in his uncle's house. Grades 4–7.

Belton, Sandra. *Ernestine and Amanda: Mysteries on Monroe Street*. New York: Simon & Schuster, 1998. 160 p. Two African-American girls find mystery in their 1950s community when a dance studio is vandalized. Grades 4–7.

Bentley, Nancy. *Writing Mysteries, Movies, Monster Stories, and More*. Brookfield, CT: Millbrook, 2001. 80 p. The basic elements of writing are clearly outlined for beginning writers. Grades 4–7.

Berends, Polly. *The Case of the Elevator Duck*. New York: Random, 1989. 60 p. An 11-year-old detective finds a duck in his apartment elevator and decides to figure out how the duck got there. Grades 2–4.

Berenstain, Stan and Jan Berenstain. *The Bear Detectives*. New York: Random, 2002. 48 p. The Bear Family become detectives to find the thief who stole a prize pumpkin. Grades K–2.
_____. *The Berenstain Bear Scouts and the Missing Merit Badge Mystery*. New York: Scholastic, 1998. 32 p. The scouts follow the clues, including some in rhyme, to determine who stole their merit badges. Grades K–2.
_____. *Berenstain Bears and No Guns Allowed*. New York: Random, 2000. 104 p. Aggressive behavior and rudeness lead to a serious discussion about violence and guns in Bear Country. Grades 3–6.

Beyer, Mark. *Secret Service*. New York: Children's Press, 2003. 48 p. Part of a series that explores the branches of federal law enforcement, this book explains how the secret service protects the president, as well as the other work performed by the agents. Grades 4–7.

Blackwood, Gary L. *Gangsters*. Tarrytown, NY: Benchmark, 2001. 72 p. Tracing the history of gangsters back to the late 19th century, the lives of Al Capone, Bonnie and Clyde, and Pretty Boy Floyd are recounted. Grades 3–6.

Bloor, Edward. *Crusader*. San Diego, CA: Harcourt, 1999. 400 p. A violent virtual reality game leads a young girl to her mother's murderer and helps her discover the difference between real and virtual worlds. Grades 9–12.

Bonsall, Crosby. *Case of the Hungry Stranger*. New York: Harper, 1992. 64 p. A private eye sets out to find out who stole a blueberry pie. Grades K–2.

Bright, Robert. *Georgie and the Robbers*. New York: Farrar, 1999. 32 p. Georgie, the gentle ghost, protects Mr. and Mrs. Whittaker's antique furniture from would-be robbers. Preschool–K.

Brooks, Kevin. *Martyn Pig*. New York: Scholastic, 2002. 240 p. When his drunken, abusive father accidentally dies, Martyn does not call anyone. An avid mystery reader, Martyn hides the body and covers his tracks. Grades 7–10.

Brooks, Walter. *Freddy the Detective*. New York: Puffin, 2001. 264 p. A porcine poetry spouting, would-be Sherlock Holmes solves a series of mysteries. Grades 3–7.

Brown, Marc. *Arthur's Mystery Envelope*. New York: Little Brown, 1998. 64 p. Arthur is curious and concerned about an enveloped marked "Confidential" that his principal asked him to deliver to his parents. Grades 2–4.

Brown, Ruth. *A Dark, Dark Tale*. New York: Puffin, 1992. The suspense will keep listeners on the edges of their seats as a cat explores a dark, dark house. Preschool–K.

Bruchac, Joseph. *Skeleton Man*. New York: Harper, 2001. 128 p. A bony guardian locks Molly in her room each night, and suspense builds as she tries to figure out why. Grades 6–9.

Bunting, Eve. *Coffin on a Case*. New York: Harper, 1993. 112 p. Henry Coffin, son of a private detective, wants a case of his own and he finds it when he helps a girl find her missing mother. Grades 3–6.
_____. *Smoky Night*. San Diego, CA: Harcourt, 1999. 36 p. Striking illustrations and a sparse storyline look at the Los Angeles riots and the impact of violence on the community. Grades K–2.

Byars, Betsy. *The Dark Stairs*. New York: Puffin, 1997. 160 p. Detecting is in Herculeah Jones' blood—her mother is a private detective and her father is a cop—and she uses her skills to solve an old murder. Grades 3–6.
_____. *Disappearing Acts*. New York: Viking, 1998. 128 p. Herculeah Jones must help her friend after he reports a missing body that has disappeared by the time the police arrive. Grades 3–7.
_____. *Wanted ... Mud Blossom*. New York: Yearling, 1993. 148 p. Pap's dog seems to have eaten the class hamster and is put on trial for the crime. Grades 3–6.

Camenson, Blythe. *Careers for Mystery Buffs and Other Snoops and Sleuths*. Columbus, OH: McGraw-Hill, 1996. 137 p. From detective to historian, careers for the curious range from the traditional to very innovative. Crime reporter, criminal psychologist, archeologist, or police officer, every mystery buff is sure to find an appealing profession. Grades 7–10.

Canterbury, Patricia E. *Carlotta's Secret*. Elk Grove, CA: RBC Publishing, 2001. 54 p. Moving from New York to the Sacramento Delta, Carlotta and the Webster Street Gang start solving mysteries. Grades 3–5.

Cheaney, J.B. *The Playmaker*. New York: Knopf, 2000. 256 p. Looking for his father in London, Richard Malory gets involved with a Shakespearian acting troupe and a secret society. Grades 6–9.

Christelow, Eileen. *Robbery at the Diamond Dog Diner*. Boston, MA: Houghton Mifflin, 1988. 32 p. Lola Dog wears her diamonds when she cooks, so she hides them when she hears that robbers are in town. Preschool–2.

Christie, Agatha. *Murder on the Orient Express.* New York: Berkley, 2000. 245 p. An American passenger is murdered on the train from Istanbul to Paris and Hercule Poirot must solve the case. Grade 9–Adult.

Claudia, Logan. *The 5,000-Year-Old Puzzle: Solving a Mystery of Ancient Egypt.* New York: Farrar, 2002. 42 p. A fictionalize account, based on actual documents and records, of a young boy's experience helping his archeologist father excavate an Egyptian tomb. Grades 1–4.

Clements, Gary. *The Great Poochini.* Toronto: Groundwood, 1999. 32 p. An opera-singing dog has a secret life and his quick thinking thwarts a burglary. Preschool–2.

Coleman, Evelyn. *Circle of Fire.* Middleton, WI: Pleasant Co., 2001. 147 p. A 12-year-old African-American girl in rural Tennessee thwarts the Klan's plans to disrupt a visit by Eleanor Roosevelt. Grades 3–6.
_____. *Mystery of the Dark Tower.* Middleton, WI: Pleasant Co., 2000. 149 p. Harlem is a lonely place for a girl from the South during the Great Migration, but Bessie must face the unknown and a mystery. Grades 3–6.

Colfer, Eoin. *Artemis Fowl.* New York: Hyperion, 2002. 277 p. Artemis is a criminal genius, and he has hatched a plot to steal the pot of gold from the fairyfolk. Grades 5–8.

Collins, Wilkie. *The Moonstone.* New York: Penguin, 1999. 528 p. A classic tale of murder, romance, and robbery, a priceless yellow diamond is stolen from an Indian temple with dire consequences. Grade 10–Adult.

Conrad, Hy. *Solve-It-Yourself Mysteries: Detective Club Puzzlers.* West Hartford, CT: Sterling Publications, 1996. 96 p. Two junior detectives show readers "who dun it" and how it was done. Grades 3–7.

Conrad, Pam. *Stonewords: A Ghost Story.* New York: Harper, 1990. 130 p. Zoe meets the ghost of another girl, also named Zoe, and travels back to 1870 to try and save her life. Grades 5–7.

Cooney, Caroline B. *Burning Up.* New York: Laurel Leaf, 2001. 230 p. Family secrets hide the truth about a fire that destroyed an apartment building in 1959. Grades 6–8.
_____. *Face on the Milk Carton.* New York: Laurel Leaf, 1991. 184 p. Janie realizes that her parents must have kidnapped her when she sees her own face on the milk carton. Grades 8–10.
_____. *What Janie Found.* New York: Laurel Leaf, 2002. 192 p. In the conclusion to the series, Cooney pulls together the story of Janie's life and the deception she has faced from her family. Grades 8–10.

Cormier, Robert. *The Rag and Bone Shop.* New York: Delacorte, 2001. 154 p. The last boy to see a seven-year-old girl before she was murdered is subjected to severe interrogation as the police attempt to quickly find the killer. Grades 6–8.

Coville, Bruce. *Ghost in the Third Row.* New York: Bantam, 1987. 134 p. Nina thinks she sees the ghost of an actress who was murdered on stage 50 years ago. Grades 4–6.

Cressy, Judith. *Can You Find It?* New York: Harry N. Abram, 2002. 40 p. This "I Spy" book invites readers to look closely at art in order to find hard-to-locate details. Grades K–2.

Cross, Gillian. *Phoning a Dead Man.* New York: Holiday House, 2002. 256 p. Hayley finds herself in danger as she investigates the accidental death of her brother. Could he have been involved with the Russian mob? Grades 6–8.

_____. *Tightrope.* New York: Holiday House, 1999. 208 p. Ashley's dual life—dream daughter and gang member—leads to threats from a mysterious stalker. Grades 7–9.

Crowe, Chris. *Getting Away with Murder: the True Story of the Emmett Till Case.* New York: Phyllis Fogelman Books, 2003. 128 p. The true story of a young Chicago boy who was murdered in Mississippi during the early days of the Civil Rights movement. Grades 6–9.

_____. *Mississippi Trial, 1955.* New York: Phyllis Fogelman Books, 2002. 231 p. A white boy visiting his grandfather in rural Mississippi confronts racism as he becomes involved in the Emmet Till lynching case in 1955. Grades 6–9.

Curtis, Jamie Lee. *Where Do Balloons Go?: an Uplifting Mystery.* New York: Harper, 2000. 36 p. In sing-song rhyme, a young boy imagines where his balloon might have gone. Preschool–K.

Cushman, Doug. *Aunt Eater Loves a Mystery.* New York: Harper, 1989. 64 p. Four short stories recount the many mysteries that Aunt Eater solves. Grades K–2.

_____. *Aunt Eater's Mystery Halloween.* New York: Harper, 1999. 64 p. Halloween provides plenty of mysteries for the amateur detective to solve. Grades K–2.

_____. *Inspector Hopper.* New York: Harper, 2000. 64 p. An insect inspector and his partner solve simple, easy-to-read mysteries. Grades K–2.

_____. *The Mystery of King Karfu.* New York: Harper, 1998. 32 p. Seymour Sleuth and his mouse assistant set out to find King Karfu's stolen stone chicken. They uncover clues, narrow down suspects, and solve the case. Preschool–1.

Dahl, Michael. *Coral Coffin.* New York: Simon & Schuster, 2001. 166 p. Finn Zwake and his mystery writer grandfather encounter modern-day pirates near the Great Barrier Reef as they continue their search for Finn's parents. Grades 4–7.

D'Angelo, Laura. *The FBI's Most Wanted.* Broomall, PA: Chelsea House, 1997. 100 p. What does it take to get on to the FBI's Most Wanted list? D'Angelo also discusses the ways that the media and the public help law enforcement agents find these fugitives. Grades 6–9.

De Capua, Sarah. *Serving on a Jury.* New York: Children's Press, 2002. 48 p. Part of the True Book series, De Capua explains the American jury system. Grades 3–6.

Deem, James M. *Bodies from the Bog.* Boston, MA: Houghton Mifflin, 1998. 48 p. The mummified body of Iron Age Man unveils the scientific mysteries of archeological science. Grades 4–7.

DeFelice, Cynthia. *Ghost of Fossil Glen.* New York: Camelot, 1999. 160 p. Hanging by her fingers from a cliff, Allie is guided to safety by a ghost that died in the glen four years earlier. Allie has been chosen to avenge the death. Grades 5–8.

_____. *Lostman's River.* New York: Avon, 1995. 160 p. Fleeing to Florida after her father murdered a man, 13-year-old Tyler learns to love the Everglades and becomes involved in a plot to steal egret feathers. Grades 3–6.

DeLaCroix, Alice. *The Hero of Third Grade.* New York: Holiday House, 2002. 96 p. Like the daring Scarlet Pimpernel in his favorite movie, Randall resolves to do good deeds and find stolen toys and other items. Grades 2–3.

Delaney, Mark. *The Kingfisher's Tale.* Atlanta, GA: Peachtree, 2000. 192 p. Four teenagers find themselves in the middle of an ecological mystery and political conspiracy when they find several dead birds. Grades 5–8.
_____. *The Vanishing Chip.* Atlanta, GA: Peachtree, 1998. 240 p. The Misfits have to find the real thief in order to clear Mattie's grandfather of charges that he stole a valuable computer chip. Grades 5–8.

Dewey, Jennifer Owings. *Finding Your Way: the Art of Natural Navigation.* Brookfield, CT: Millbrook, 2001. 64 p. Clues and hints are available wherever you are, if you know how to look for them and learn to trust your instincts. Grades 3–7.

Dexter, Catherine. *I Dream of Murder.* New York: Morrow, 1997. 155 p. Jere is haunted by dreams where he sees a murder replayed over and over again. Grades 4–6.

Dixon, Franklin W. *The Tower Treasure.* New York: Grosset & Dunlap, 1976. 180 p. A dying criminal confesses that he has stashed his loot in a tower. Originally published in 1927, this is the first in the Hardy Boys series. Grades 3–6.

Donnelly, Jennifer. *A Northern Light.* San Diego, CA: Harcourt, 2003. 396 p. Mattie faces a tough life but dreams of going to school in New York City. Set in 1906, Mattie's story becomes interwoven with the murder of a young girl—the true case that inspired *An American Tragedy.* Grades 8–12.

Doyle, Arthur Conan. *The Adventures of Sherlock Holmes.* New York: Morrow, 1992. 342 p. The first 12 cases of Sherlock Holmes are illustrated by Barry Moser. Grades 3–8.
_____. *The Complete Sherlock Holmes: All 4 Novels and 56 Short Stories.* New York: Bantam, 1998. 944 p. Four novels and 56 short stories that feature Sherlock Holmes provide the canon in one extensive volume. Grades 8–Adult.

Duffey, Betsy. *Camp Knock Knock Mystery.* New York: Yearling, 1997. 47 p. Willie's prized book of knock-knock jokes is missing and readers have to follow the visual clues and riddles to solve the crime. Grades 1–3.

Duncan, Lois. *Don't Look Behind You.* New York: Laurel Leaf, 1990. 176 p. Her comfortable life turns topsy-turvy when April's father enters the a federal witness protection plan, but is her life in danger? Grades 7–10.
_____. *Down a Dark Hall.* New York: Laurel Leaf, 1997. 192 p. Fourteen-year-old Kit realizes that she is in danger as she figures out why she was selected to attend a prestigious boarding school. Grades 7–10.

_____. *Killing Mr. Griffin*. New York: Laurel Leaf, 1993. 223 p. Although they only planned to scare their teacher, a group of students kill him and then try to cover up their crime while dealing with their guilt. Grades 7–10.

_____. *Who Killed My Daughter?* New York: Dell, 1994. 354 p. A mother searches for her daughter's killer in a true crime tale that is very personal to this famous mystery writer. Grades 10–Adult.

Durrett, Deanne. *Unsung Heroes of World War II: The Story of the Navajo Code Talkers*. New York: Facts on File, 1998. 128 p. Using their own language as a secret code, Navajo Marines contributed to U.S. efforts to win World War II. Grades 6–10.

Egan, Tim. *The Blunder of the Rogues*. Boston, MA: Houghton Mifflin, 1999. 32 p. The Rogues are a motley group of friends who embark on a life of crime, but a short stint in prison helps the friends mend their ways. Preschool–1.

Erickson, John. *The Original Adventures of Hank the Cowdog*. New York: Puffin, 1999. 136 p. Hank is the number one suspect in the murder he is investigating on the ranch. Grades 3–6.

Ericson, Helen. *Harriet Spies Again*. New York: Delacorte, 2002. 230 p. When Harriet's parents go to Paris for three months, Ole Golly returns to care for her and Harriet is determined to find out why her beloved Nanny has returned. Grades 4–7.

Eth, Clifford. *Flatfoot Fox and the Case of the Missing Schoolhouse*. Boston, MA: Houghton Mifflin, 1997. 48 p. Flatfoot Fox and Secretary Bird have a Holmes/Watson relationship, but their talents are put to the test when Wacky Weasel makes the school disappear. Grades 2–4.

Ferguson, Dwayne J. *Kid Caramel Private Investigator: The Case of the Missing Ankh*. East Orange, NJ: Just Us Books, 1997. 64 p. The fifth-grade detective works with the police to solve a mystery at the art museum. Grades 3–6.

Ferris, Jean. *Love Among the Walnuts: Or How I Saved My Entire Family from Being Poisoned*. New York: Puffin, 2001. 216 p. Two money grubbing uncles try to poison Sandy and his family and Sandy is determined to bring them to justice. Grades 3–6.

Fields, Terri. *After the Death of Anna Gonzales*. New York: Holt, 2002. 112 p. Forty-seven poems tell the story of a young girl's suicide and the clues she leaves tell the story of her life. Grades 7–12.

Fitzgerald, John D. *The Great Brain*. New York: Dial, 2000. 175 p. Known as the Great Brain, 10-year-old Tom D. Fitzgerald faces many adventures as a con artist in the early 1900s. Grades 2–5.

Fitzhugh, Louise. *Harriet the Spy*. New York: Yearling, 2001. 300 p. Harriet finds herself a lonely outcast when her friends find the notebook where she has recorded their secrets. Grades 4–7.

Fleischman, Sid. *Bo & Mzzz Mad.* New York: Greenwillow, 2001. 112 p. Sent to live with relatives who have been feuding for generations, 12-year-old Bo faces a con artist, a treasure map, and a crime spree. Grades 3–6.

_____. *Disappearing Act.* Greenwillow, 2003. 133 p. When their parents disappear, Kevin and his sister flee to California trying to stay ahead of a stalker by taking on new identities. Grades 5–7.

Fridell, Ron. *DNA Fingerprinting: the Ultimate Identity.* New York: Watts, 2001. 112 p. Clearly explaining the science of DNA, Fridell explores its role in solving contemporary crimes and clearing up historical mysteries. Grades 6–9.

_____. *Solving Crimes: Pioneers of Forensic Science.* New York: Watts, 2000. 144 p. Cases and the people who pioneered the scientific techniques to solve crimes are detailed in readable sections. Grades 7–12.

_____. *Spying: The Modern World of Espionage.* Brookfield, CT: Twenty-First Century Books, 2002. 144 p. The basics of modern espionage, and the failures and successes of intelligence, are clearly explained and the technologies explored. Grades 7–12.

Friedlander, Jr., Mark P. and Terry M. Phillips. *When Objects Talk: Solving a Crime with Science.* Minneapolis, MN: Lerner, 2001. 120 p. Using a fictional murder case, the authors explain the scientific principles and techniques used to bring the culprit to justice. Grades 4–7.

Fritz, Jean. *Traitor: the Case of Benedict Arnold.* New York: Putnam, 1981. 191 p. A compelling biography of one of America's greatest traitors explores the twists in Arnold's life that led him from heroism to treason. Grades 3–7.

Galdone, Joanna. *The Tailypo!: a Ghost Story.* Boston, MA: Houghton Mifflin, 1984. 32 p. A strange varmint haunts the woodsman who cut off his tail. Preschool–1.

Gantos, Jack. *A Hole in My Life.* New York: Farrar, 2002. 208 p. At 20, author Jack Gantos went to prison for drug smuggling. With bold and disturbing honesty, Gantos tells how he turned his life around. Grades 8–12.

Garfield, Leon. *The December Rose.* New York: Viking, 1989. 208 p. A young chimney sweep in Victorian London overhears a conspiracy and becomes involved in espionage and adventure. Grades 4–7.

Geisert, Arthur. *Nursery Crimes.* Boston, MA: Houghton Mifflin, 2001. 32 p. When a topiary turkey is stolen right before Thanksgiving, Jambo and Marva follow the clues to find the thief. Preschool–2.

George, Jean Craighead. *The Case of the Missing Cutthroats.* New York: Harper, 1999. 160 p. Spinner and her cousin catch a fish that is supposed to be extinct. Grades 3–6.

_____. *The Fire Bug Connection.* New York: Harper, 1995. 148 p. While at an environmental camp, 12-year-old Maggie can't figure out why lighting bugs are dying. Grades 3–7.

_____. *Who Really Killed Cock Robin?* New York: Harper, 1992. 208 p. Foul play is suspected when the town mascot, a robin named Cock Robin, dies. Tony, an eighth grader who is an expert on robins, is called in to investigate. Grades 4–8.

Gerdes, Louise, ed. *Serial Killers*. San Diego, CA: Greenhaven, 2000. 192 p. This Contemporary Issues Companion book pulls information from diverse sources to profile serial killers and their characteristics. Grades 10–12.

Gibbons, Gail. *Pirates*. New York: Little Brown, 1999. 32 p. The truth about pirates is explored, from their swashbuckling antics to biographies of infamous pirates and notes about still-buried treasures. Grades 2–4.

Giff, Patricia Reilly. *Kidnap at the Catfish Café*. New York: Viking, 1998. 80 p. Minnie rescues a cat and names him Max. Together they become involved in the search for the owner of an amber ring. Grades 3–6.

Gilbert, Barbara Snow. *Paper Trail*. Asheville, NC: Front Page, 2000. 168 p. Factual research combines with a gripping story about a boy who is running from a para-military group. Grades 8–10.

Giles, Gail. *Dead Girls Don't Write Letters*. Brookfield, CT: Roaring Brook, 2003. 136 p. A stranger shows up claiming to be Sunny's sister, who died in a fire five months earlier. Grades 5–8.

Glass, Andrew. *Bad Guys: True Stories of Legendary Gunslingers*. New York: Doubleday, 1998. 48 p. A quick look at eight of the orneriest men and women of the Wild West, including Billy the Kid and Jesse James. Grades 3–5.

Glenn, Mel. *Foreign Exchange: a Mystery in Poems*. New York: Morrow, 1999. 160 p. Pairing urban kids with small town teens leads to murder and the suspect is an African-American boy who danced with the victim. Stereotypes and prejudice are explored through poetry and mystery. Grades 8–12.
_____. *The Taking of Room 114: A Hostage Drama in Poems*. New York: Lodestar, 1997. A berserk teacher takes his senior class hostage, and the students, parents, police, and other teachers reveal their feelings, thoughts, and concerns through poetry. Grades 8–12.
_____. *Who Killed Mr. Chippendale?: A Mystery in Poems*. New York: Puffin, 1999. 112 p. Told in free form poetry, this mystery explores the murder of a popular teacher. Grades 8–12.

Gliori, Debi. *Pure Dead Magic*. New York: Knopf, 2002. 224 p. Signor Luciano Strega-Borgia is kidnapped and his children try to find him in this "cyber-gothic" fantasy. Grades 6–8.

Gree, Gary and Rob Ruddick. *Billy the Ghost and Me*. New York: Harper, 1997. 47 p. Sarah and her friend, Billy the ghost, outwit bank robbers in a western town in this slapstick tale of adventure. Grades 1–3.

Greene, Stephanie. *Owen Foote, Super Spy*. Boston, MA: Clarion, 2001. 96 p. Owen loves to play super-spy and he is adept at using codes, but his cloak and dagger exploits land him in some hilarious situations. Grades 3–6.

Griffin, Peni. *The Ghost Sitter*. New York: Puffin, 2002. 144 p. Susie does not understand why her family has left her behind when they moved away because she does not know that she is dead. Grades 4–6.

Guiberson, Brenda Z. *Mummy Mysteries from North America*. New York: Henry Holt, 1998. 64 p. True tales of North American mummies and the ancient mysteries they solve are told in simple chapters. Grades 2–5.

Hale, Bruce. *The Chameleon Wore Chartreuse*. San Diego, CA: Harcourt, 2001. 120 p. A fourth-grade gumshoe and his sidekick search for a missing chameleon in this hard-boiled mystery. Grades 3–6.

Hamilton, Virginia. *House of Dies Drear*. New York: Pocket Book, 1984. 256 p. An old house has secret tunnels and buried treasure, but the real mystery is whether it is haunted by the ghosts of abolitionists and runaway slaves. Grades 4–7.
_____. *The Mystery of Drear House*. New York: Scholastic, 1997. 224 p. The treasure of Drear House is found, but to whom does it belong? Grades 4–7.

Hart, Alison. *Chase: a Police Story*. New York: Random, 2002. 96 p. State police are on the look-out for an escaped convict. When he is spotted in Staunton, Virginia, a chase ensues. Grades 3–6.
_____. *Rescue*. New York: Random, 2002. 96 p. Armed bank robbers take hostages in this mystery based on real cases from the Staunton, Virginia, Police Department. Grades 3–6.

Hass, Elizabeth. *Incognito Mosquito, Private Insective*. New York: Random, 1989. 96 p. A private "insective" gets caught in sticky situations when he sets out to solve crimes. Full of puns and fun. Grades 2–4.

Hautman, Pete. *Mr. Was*. New York: Simon & Schuster, 1996. 216 p. Jack meets his grandfather for the first time and the old man tries to kill him, setting into motion a sophisticated time-travel mystery. Grades 6–9.

Hawes, Charles Boardman. *The Dark Frigate*. New York: Little Brown, 1996. 246 p. Plucked from a floating wreck, Phillip is forced to join a band of pirates. Grades 6–9.

Hearne, Betsy. *Who's In the Hall?: a Mystery in Four Chapters*. New York: Greenwillow, 2000. 32 p. An urban apartment building offers entertaining mysteries told through rhyming verse and tongue-twisters. Grades K–3.

Hiaasen, Carl. *Hoot*. New York: Knopf, 2002. 292 p. He has no friends in his new school, but Roy Eberhardt finds himself involved in a mystery and eco-adventures. Grades 5–8.

Hildick, E.W. *The Case of the Wiggling Wig*. New York: Simon & Schuster, 1996. 154 p. The 25th case that McGurk will solve may also be his most hair-raising! Grades 3–6.

Hoban, Lillian. *The Case of the Two Masked Robbers*. New York: Harper, 1988. 64 p. The raccoon twins track down the robbers who stole Mrs. Turtle's eggs. Grades 2–4.

Hobbs, Will. *Ghost Canoe*. New York: Camelot, 1998. 208 p. Nathan not only solves a murder and brings the killer to justice, he also finds the treasure and solves the mystery of the Indian canoe and skeleton he finds hanging in a treetop. Grades 5–8.

Horowitz, Anthony. *Stormbreaker*. New York: Putnam, 2002. 208 p. Fourteen-year-old Alex is a superspy recruited to find the man who killed his uncle. Grades 6–9.

Howe, James. *Bunnicula: A Rabbit-Tale of Mystery*. New York: Aladdin, 1996. 96 p. The Monroe family finds a bunny and mysterious things begin to happen. Grades 3–6.
_____. *Nighty-Nightmare*. New York: Aladdin, 1997. 129 p. Bunnicula, Howie, Harold, and the Monroe family face a night of terror when they camp next to two strange men and then listen to Chester's horrifying tales. Grades 3–6.

Howe, Norma. *The Blue Avenger Cracks the Code*. New York: Harper, 2002. 368 p. A 16-year-old self-made superhero is on the case to track down the true author of Shakespeare's plays and save the world from crime. Grades 6–10.

Hurd, Thatcher. *Art Dog*. New York: Harper, 1998. 32 p. A guard at the Art Museum, Arthur Dog leads a quiet life except when the moon is full and he finds himself in the middle of an art heist. Preschool–3.
_____. *Mystery on the Docks*. New York: Harper, 1984. 32 p. A short-order cook rescues a kidnapped opera singer. Preschool–2.

Jackson, Donna M. *The Bone Detectives: How Forensic Anthropologists solve Crimes and Uncover Mysteries of the Dead*. New York: Little Brown, 1996. 48 p. A forensic anthropologist explains how bones and other clues are used to identify the victim of a crime and help find her killer. Grades 3–7.
_____. *The Wildlife Detectives: How Forensic Scientists Fight Crimes Against Nature*. Boston, MA: Houghton Mifflin, 2000. 48 p. Using details of an actual case, Jackson explains how scientists examine clues and follow tips to solve crimes against wild animals. Grades 3–6.

Jeffery, Laura S. *Simon Wiesenthal: Tracking Down Nazi Criminals*. Berkeley Heights, NJ: Enslow, 1997. 104 p. A biography of the famous Nazi hunter, the stories tell how war criminals were located and brought to justice through careful record keeping and tenacity. Grades 6–9.

Jones, Charlotte Foltz. *Fingerprints and Talking Bones: How Real-Life Crimes are Solved*. New York: Bantam, 1997. 112 p. (out of print) Without being gory or gross, Jones describes and explains police forensic science. Grades 4–6.

Joosse, Barbara. *Stars in the Darkness*. San Francisco, CA: Chronicle, 2002. 36 p. A young boy tells how his brother became a "gang-banger" and explains the actions that he and his mother take to make their neighborhood peaceful. Preschool–2.

Josephson, Judith Pinkerton. *Allan Pinkerton: The Original Private Eye*. Minneapolis, MN: Lerner, 1996. 124 p. The life of North America's most famous private detective is explored through primary documents, journals, letters, and photographs. Grades 6–9.

Kastner, Erich. *Emil and the Detectives*. New York: Scholastic, 1985. 160 p. Vintage mystery, this book is considered to be the first mystery written specifically for young readers. Twelve-year-old Emil traps a pickpocket. Grades 3–7.

Katz, Welwyn Wilton. *False Face.* Toronto: Groundwood, 1987. 155 p. Thirteen-year-old Laney finds two Iroquois masks in a bog and gets involved in a mystery that makes her question love and hatred. Grades 4–7.

Keene, Carolyn. *The Secret of the Old Clock.* New York: Price Stern Sloane, 1930. 180 p. Nancy Drew has to solve the mystery of an old man's will. Grades 3–7.

Kehret, Peg. *Don't Tell Anyone.* New York: Puffin, 2001. 144 p. Megan witnesses a hit-and-run accident and becomes involved in a criminal's plan to embezzle money when she tries to save feral cats on a construction site. Grades 3–6.
_____. *Spy Cat.* New York: Dutton, 2003. 192 p. The Kendrill family is concerned about burglaries in their neighborhood, but Pete, a watch cat, is sure he can protect his family. Grades 4–7.

Kellogg, Steven. *The Missing Mitten Mystery.* New York: Puffin, 2002. 32 p. Annie has to retrace her steps to locate a missing mitten. Preschool–1.

Kerr, M.E. *What Became of Her?* New York: Harper, 2002. 256 p. A wealthy young woman returns to her family home to settle the score with those who taunted her as a child. Grades 6–9.

Kevi. *Don't Talk to Strangers.* New York: Scholastic, 2003. 32 p. Rapper Kevi Kev uses catchy rhymes to help children understand the dangers of strangers and how to avoid trouble. Grades 1–4.

Kimmel, Eric. *The Erie Canal Pirates.* New York: Holiday House, 2002. 32 p. Inspired by a folksong, Captain Flynn and his crew are besieged by pirates on the inland canal. Preschool–2.

Kitamura, Staoshi. *Sheep in Wolves' Clothing.* New York: Farrar, 1996. 40 p. Having shed their wool coats in order to go swimming, three sheep hire a detective to help locate the conniving wolves that stole the coats. Preschool–2.

Klause, Annette Curtis. *Alien Secrets.* New York: Yearling, 1995. 240 p. Expelled from boarding school, 12-year-old Puck leaves Earth and befriends an alien when a murder occurs on the space ship. Grades 5–7.

Klise, Kate. *Letters from Camp.* New York: Avon, 1999. 179 p. Three sets of kids are supposed to learn how to get along at Camp Harmony but instead find themselves involved in a series of criminal activities. Told through letters. Grades 4–7.
_____. *Regarding the Fountain: a Tale, in Letters, of Liars and Leaks.* New York: Avon, 1999. 144 p. Told entirely through letters and faxes, fifth-grade students discover a dirty secret as they build a water fountain. Grades 4–7.
_____. *Trial by ~~Jury~~ Journal.* New York: Harper, 2002. 256 p. Lily is the first juvenile juror and she finds herself sequestered in a hotel. Grades 4–6.

Konigsburg, E.L. *From the Mixed-up Files of Mrs. Basil E. Frankweiler.* New York: Yearling, 1977. 162 p. Twelve-year-old Claudia Kincaid runs away and becomes involved in a mystery in the Metropolitan Museum of Art. Grades 4–7.

_____. *Up from Jericho Tel.* New York: Atheneum, 1986. 178 p. The ghost of a once-famous actress helps Jeanmarie and Malcolm find a missing necklace. Grades 4–7.

Korman, Gordon. *Son of the Mob.* New York: Hyperion, 2002. 272 p. Vince Luca is a regular high-school guy, except that his dad is the head of the mob. This is helpful for getting good grades but disastrous for dating, especially when the girl's dad is an FBI agent! Grades 7–10.

Kotzwinkle, William. *Trouble in Bugland: A Collection of Inspector Mantis Mysteries.* Boston, MA: Godine, 1996. 190 p. Praying Mantis and his sidekick Dr. Hopper embark on a series of Holmes-style mystery investigations. Grades 3–6.

Kraft, Betsy Harvey. *Sensational Trials of the 20th Century.* New York: Scholastic, 1998. 208 p. Eight famous legal battles, from *Brown v. Board of Education* to the O.J. Simpson murder trial, are examined. Grades 4–7.

Krentsky, Stephen. *The Three Blind Mice Mystery.* New York: Yearling, 1995. 46 p. Detective Simple Simon tries to find a blind mouse, but a ferocious wolf is on the loose and two pigs are having trouble with their houses. Grades 2–4.

Kupperberg, Paul. *Spy Satellites.* New York: Rosen, 2003. 64 p. Spy satellites tend to be top-secret, but declassified information and expert opinions provide an intriguing look at the technology and policies of spying from the sky. Grades 4–6.

Labatt, Mary. *Aliens in Woodford.* Tonawanda, NY: Kids Can Press, 2000. 116 p. Sam, the talking sheepdog detective, investigates the mysterious disappearance of neighborhood pets. Grades 3–6.

Laden, Nina. *Private I. Guana: The Case of the Missing Chameleon.* San Francisco, CA: Chronicle, 1995. 32 p. It is hard to find a missing chameleon, especially when he keeps turning colors and blending with the surroundings. Preschool–1.

Landon, Lucinda. *Meg Mackintosh and the Mystery in the Locked Library.* North Scituate, RI: Secret Passage Press, 1996. 43 p. Meg tries to find a rare book that was stolen from the library. Grades 3–6 .

_____. *Meg Mackintosh and the Mystery of Camp Creepy.* North Scituate, RI: Secret Passage Press, 1997. 64 p. Meg has until sundown to solve a puzzle prepared by one of the camp counselors. Grades 3–6.

Lane, Brian. *Crimebusters: The Investigation of Murder.* Brookfield, CT: Copper Beech Books, 1996. 32 p. Using a real murder as the basis for investigation, the facts are highlighted so that readers test their own investigative skills. Grades 3–6.

Lasky, Kathryn. *Alice Rose and Sam.* New York: Hyperion, 1998. 208 p. Alice Rose develops a friendship with Samuel Clemens and helps him solve a Civil War murder mystery. (Available from Recorded Books.) Grades 3–6.

_____. *Shadows in the Water.* San Diego, CA: Harcourt, 1992. 211 p. The Starbuck twins find a mystery in the Florida Keys as they investigate toxic waste. Grades 3–6.

Lass, Bonnie. *Who Took the Cookies from the Cookie Jar?* New York: Little Brown, 2000. 32 p. Various animals are portrayed as the cookie thieves in this traditional rhyming game, but Skunk is trying to solve the mystery. Preschool–K.

Lawrence, Caroline. *The Pirates of Pompeii.* Brookfield, CT: Roaring Brook, 2002. 160 p. Children are disappearing from the refugee camps following the eruption of Vesuvius. The trail leads Flavia to pirates and slave traders in the Ancient Roman world. Grades 4–6.

_____. *The Thieves of Ostia.* Brookfield, CT: Roaring Brook, 2002. 160 p. Flavia Gemina, the daughter of a sea captain, is an accomplished amateur detective in the Ancient Roman city of Ostia. Grades 4–6.

Leroe, Ellen. *Ghost Dog.* New York: Hyperion, 1993. 64 p. A poltergeist pug helps Artie recover his grandfather's stolen baseball card. Grades 2–4.

Lester, Julius. *When Dad Killed Mom.* San Diego, CA: Harcourt, 2001. 176 p. Domestic violence leads to a family tragedy, and two teens must re-create a family of their own after their father kills their mother. Grades 8–12.

LeValliant, Ted & Marcel Theroux. *What's the Verdict?: You're the Judge in 90 Tricky Courtroom Quizzes.* West Hartford, CT: Sterling Publications, 1991. 128 p. Legal puzzles based on real cases let readers match wits with the court. Grades 4–7.

LeVert, Marianne. *Crime.* New York: Facts on File, 1991. 149 p. A look at the factors affecting crime in America and the causes of juvenile crime. Grades 5–9.

Levin, Betty. *Shadow-Catcher.* New York: Harper, 2000. 160 p. A stranger shows undue interest in the photographs Jonathan and his grandfather took of a river accident, leading them to believe it might not have been an accident after all. Grades 5–8.

Levy, Elizabeth. *The Creepy Computer Mystery.* New York: Cartwheel, 1996. 46 p. A famous writer disappears in the middle of an online chat sessions and a trio of kids, who call themselves Invisible Ink, are on the case. Grades K–2.

_____. *The Mystery of the Missing Dog.* New York: Scholastic, 1995. (unpaged). An invisible boy loses his invisible dog, but along with his friends, a team of detectives, Chip is hot on the trail of dognappers. Grades 1–3.

_____. *Something Queer is Going On.* New York: Delacorte, 1977. 48 p. When Fletcher disappears Jill is certain that her basset hound has been stolen. Grades 1–4.

Logan, Claudia. *The 5,000-Year-Old Puzzle.* New York: Farrar, 2002. 48 p. Rich collages and replicas of documents and artifacts are arranged in diary format as a young boy explores the pyramids in Giza. Grades 2–6.

Lourie, Peter. *The Lost Treasure of Captain Kidd*. Honesdale, PA: Boyds Mills, 1996. 94 p. A pirate legend, a treasure hunt, and ghosts bring together two boys living along the Hudson River. Grades 3–6.

Mahr, Juli. *Mailbox Mice Mystery*. New York: Random, 1999. 32 p. Clues in envelopes addressed to Watson Mouse help him discover who stole the cheese in this interactive book. Grades 2–3.

Marrina, Albert. *Terror of the Spanish Main: Sir Henry Morgan and his Buccaneers*. New York: Dutton, 1999. 224 p. Recreating the 17th century world in which Sir Henry Morgan was raised, Marrin explores the often conflicting sides of this notorious pirate. Grades 7–12.

Marzollo, Jane. *I Spy Mystery: a Book of Picture Riddles*. New York: Cartwheel, 1993. 37 p. Readers have to look carefully to find common objects hidden in the colorful photographs. Preschool–K.

Mayo, Margaret. *Emergency!* Minneapolis, MN: Carolrhoda, 2002. 32 p. Sirens wail as emergency vehicles rush to help those in need. Preschool–1.

McClements, George. *Jake Gander, Storyville Detective: The Case of the Greedy Granny*. New York: Hyperion, 2002. 32 p. Jake Gander takes on a case for Red R. Hood who is suspicious about her grandmother's activities. Grades 1–4.

McGraw, Eloise Jarvis. *Mara, Daughter of the Nile*. New York: Viking, 1990. 279 p. Mara, an Egyptian slave girl, uses her skill in reading hieroglyphics to become a spy. Grades 3–6.

McGraw, Eloise. *The Golden Goblet*. New York: Puffin, 1990. 248 p. Ranofer is trying to become a master goldsmith but has to thwart the criminal plotting of his evil uncle in order to succeed. Grades 3–6.

Medearis, Angela Shelf. *The Ghost of Sifty-Sifty Sam*. New York: Scholastic, 1997. 40 p. Sam haunts an East Texas mansion until Chef Dan makes it through one frightful night and breaks the curse. Preschool–2.
_____. *The Spray Paint Mystery*. Little Apple, 1996. 102 p. Like his detective father, Cameron collects evidence to find the person who is spray-painting the school walls. Grades 3–5.

Melton, H. Keith. *The Ultimate Spy Book*. New York: DK Publishing, 1996. 176 p. Co-written with former CIA director William Colby, this book explores every aspect of the secret world of espionage. Grades 4–7.

Meltzer, Milton. *Case Closed: The Real Scoop on Detective Work*. New York: Scholastic, 2001. 96 p. The workday world of police investigation and tools from the Pinkertons to DNA are clearly explained. Grades 3–6.

Miklowitz, Gloria D. *Camouflage*. San Diego, CA: Harcourt, 1998. 208 p. A Los Angeles teenager flees his mother to live with his father, only to learn that dad is in a secret militia that plans to blow up a federal building. Grades 6–8.

Mitchell, Marianne. *Finding Zola.* Honesdale, PA: Boyds Mills, 2003. 144 p. Confined to a wheelchair after an accident that killed her father, Crystal is forced to deal with two mysteries that may change her life. Grades 5–8.

Mukerji, Dhan Gopal. *Gay Neck: the Story of a Pigeon.* New York: Dutton, 1968. 191 p. A carrier pigeon ferries messages for the Bengal Regiment in World War I. Grades 3–7.

Myers, Walter Dean. *Monster.* New York: Harper, 1999. 288 p. On trial for murder, a Harlem teen describes the drama of his ordeal in the form of a screenplay. Grades 9–12.

_____. *Sniffy Blue: Ace Crime Detective.* New York: Scholastic, 1999. 80 p. Smiffy's slapstick style of investigating turns crime solving into a humorous adventure. Grades 1–4.

Naylor, Phyllis Reynolds. *The Treasure of Bessledorf Hill.* New York: Simon & Schuster, 1999. 127 p. Officer Feeney thinks that a pirate hid his treasure in Middleburg and Bernie sets out to help solve the mystery. Grades 5–7.

Newman, Robert. *Case of the Baker Street Irregular.* New York: Macmillan, 1978. 216 p. Andrew gets a job working for Sherlock Holmes and gets caught up in a series of crimes. Grades 5–7.

Nickerson, Sara. *How to Disappear Completely and Never Be Found.* New York: Harper, 2002. 282 p. An off-beat mystery that involves comic books and coincidences to solve the mystery about how a young girl's father died. Grades 5–7.

Nilsen, Anna. *Art Fraud Detective: Spot the Differences, Solve the Crime!* Boston, MA: Kingfisher, 2000. 48 p. Split pages are used to tell a mystery story, play a spot-the-differences game, and learn about art. Grades 2–5.

Nixon, Joan Lowery. *Don't Scream.* New York: Bantam, 1997. 165 p. Jess investigates the new neighbors, only to learn that they are in the federal witness protection program and a psychopath is trying to find them. Grades 5–8.

_____. *Gus and Gertie and the Missing Pearl.* New York: SeaStar, 2000. 48 p. A penguin couple becomes involved in a mystery when they arrive for an island holiday. Grades 1–4.

_____. *The Name of the Game was Murder.* New York: Laurel Leaf, 1994. 182 p. Augustus Trevor blackmails a group of celebrities into playing a deadly game at his mansion, but when he is bludgeoned to death, Samantha is challenged to find his murderer. Grades 5–8.

_____. *The Search for the Shadowman.* New York: Yearling, 1998. 149 p. Andy's school assignment, to research something about his family, reveals shameful secrets. Grades 4–8.

_____. *The Stalker.* New York: Laurel Leaf, 1987. 192 p. Jessica's best friend's mother has been murdered. As she sets out to prove that her friend is innocent, Jessica finds herself in danger. Grades 5–8.

_____. *Who Are You?* New York: Delacorte, 1999. 192 p. Who is the man who has been keeping a secret file on Kristi and is her life in danger? Grades 6–9.

Nodset, Joan. *Who Took the Farmers Hat?* New York: Harper, 1998. 32 p. No one has seen the farmer's hat and none of the animals can figure out where it has gone. Preschool–1.

Obrist, Jurg. *Max and Molly and the Mystery of the Missing Honey.* New York: North South, 2001. 48 p. Two bears are accused of stealing their grandfather's honey and must catch the real thief to clear their name and solve the crime. Grades K–2.

Osborne, Mary Pope. *Mummies in the Morning.* New York: Random, 1993. 65 p. Jack and Annie go back to Ancient Egypt to help Queen Hutep find her copy of the *Book of the Dead.* Grades 2–4.

_____. *Pirates Past Noon.* New York: Random, 1994. 67 p. The Magic Tree House takes Jack and Annie back to an island filled with ruthless pirates. Grades 2–4.

_____. *Stage Fright on a Summer Night.* New York: Random, 2002. 96 p. A mysterious rhyme from Morgan Le Fay sends Jack and Annie back to Shakespearean England. Grades 2–4.

Owen, David. *Police Lab: How Forensic Science Tracks Down and Convicts Criminals.* Toronto: Firefly, 2002. 128 p. History and forensics are combined to explore several infamous murders and mysteries, including the Kennedy assassination and the Bundy murders. Grades 6–12.

Palatini, Margie. *The Web Files.* New York: Hyperion, 2001. 32 p. Paying homage to Dragnet, two duck-tectives attempt to "quack the cases" they are investigating. Preschool–2.

Pearce, Philippa. *Familiar and Haunting: Collected Stories.* New York: Greenwillow, 2002. 392 p. Thirty-seven short stories that offer mysterious, strange, and sad tales that will haunt readers. Grades 4–8.

Pearson, Mary E. *Scribbler of Dreams.* San Diego, CA: Harcourt, 2002. 240 p. Two families, the Crutchfields and the Malones, have hated each other for generations, but Kait falls in love with a Crutchfield boy. Grades 6–8.

Peck, Richard. *Are You in the House Alone?* New York: Puffin, 2000. 160 p. Notes and frightening phone calls cause a young girl to fear for her life. Grades 8–12.

Peretti, Frank. *Hangman's Curse.* Nashville, TN: Tommy Nelson, 2002. 288 p. As members of a top-secret presidential investigative team, the Veritas Project, Elisha and Elijah and their parents investigate a mysterious ailment that has stricken three athletes. Grades 4–9.

_____. *The Door in the Dragon's Throat.* Wheaton, IL: Good News, 1990. 125 p. The Copper Kids help their archeologist father and become involved in Indiana Jones-style adventures. Grades 3–6.

Phillips, Kathleen C. *How to Write a Story.* New York: Watts, 1995. 160 p. From idea to editing, this book explains how to write a story. Grades 5–7.

Plum-Ucci, Carol. *Body of Christopher Creed.* San Diego, CA: Harcourt, 2000. 248 p. After the town outcast disappears without a trace, 16-year-old Torey Adam's finds his life changed as he deals with the fact that some mysteries are never solved. Grades 7–12.

Poe, Edgar Allan. *Tales of Edgar Allan Poe.* New York: Morrow, 1991. 308 p. Eighteen of Poe's most chilling and macabre tales are illustrated by Barry Moser. Grades 3–7.

Preller, James. *The Case of the Ghostwriter.* New York: Little Apple, 2001. 80 p. Theodore Jones, known as Jigsaw, is hired to find the identity of the mystery writer who will be visiting the second-grade class.
_____. *The Case of the Secret Valentine.* New York: Scholastic, 1999. 80 p. Second-grade sleuth Jigsaw Jones solves a Valentine's Day mystery. Grades 2–3.

Pullman, Philip. *The Ruby in the Smoke.* New York: Random, 1994. 230 p. Sixteen-year-old Sally Lockhart becomes involved in a deadly web of events as she searches for a mysterious ruby in Victorian England. Grades 6–9.

Pyle, Howard. *The Book of Pirates.* Mineola, NY: Dover, 2000. 320 p. This classic assortment of pirate stories features the marauding exploits of pirates and buccaneers. Grades 6–9.

Quackenbush, Robert. *Two Miss Mallard Mysteries.* New York: Quackenbush Studios, 1998. 64 p. *Surfboard in Peril* and *Stage Door to Terror* are reprinted to share the exploits of the world's greatest duck-tective. Grades 2–4.

Qualey, Marsha. *Close to a Killer.* New York: Delacorte, 1999. 182 p. The only connection between two people who were murdered is her mother's hair salon. Barrie has to find the real killer to prove that her mother isn't the murderer. Grades 8–12.

Quinlan, Susan E. *The Case of the Mummified Pigs and Other Mysteries in Nature.* Honesdale, PA: Boyds Mills, 1999. 128 p. Fourteen ecological mysteries are explored by scientists. Grades 4–6.

Raskin, Ellen. *The Mysterious Disappearance of Leon (I Mean Noel).* New York: Viking, 1989. 148 p. Mrs. Dumpling Carillon is searching for her husband, Leon. Various clues help readers solve the puzzle along with Tina and Tony. Grades 3–7.
_____. *The Westing Game.* New York: Dutton, 1978. 185 p. Sixteen heirs must solve a puzzle or they won't inherit the money. Grades 4–8.

Rathman, Peggy. *Officer Buckle and Gloria.* New York: Putnam, 1995. Gloria, the police dog, helps spice up Officer Buckle's school safety programs. Preschool–3.

Reiss, Kathryn. *Paperquake: A Puzzle.* San Diego, CA: Harcourt, 2002. 288 p. Violet, the non-identical triplet, feels left out until she stumbles upon a 1906 diary and letters about three people caught in the 1906 San Francisco earthquake. Grades 4–8.

Rinaldi, Ann. *The Coffin Quilt: The Feud Between the Hatfields and the McCoys.* New York: Gulliver, 2001. 228 p. Fanny McCoy lives with the age-old feud between her family and the Hatfield family in the mountains of Kentucky. Grades 5–8.

Roberts, Willo Davis. *Baby-Sitting is a Dangerous Job.* New York: Fawcett, 1987. 161 p. Three bratty kids are kidnapped while 13-year-old Darcy is babysitting. Grades 3–6.

_____. *Megan's Island*. New York: Aladdin, 1990. 187 p. Three strangers are spying on Megan and her family and the danger seems to be linked to a family secret. Grades 3–6.

_____. *The Pet-Sitting Peril*. New York: Aladdin, 1990. 167 p. While doing odd jobs, a young boy learns about an arsonist's plot to torch the building. Grades 3–6.

_____. *View from the Cherry Tree*. New York: Simon & Schuster, 1975. 192 p. Rob retreats from family turmoil to his favorite hiding place only to witness a murder. Grades 4–7.

Rocklin, Joanne. *Case of the Backyard Treasure*. New York: Cartwheel, 1998. 48 p. Liz the Whiz follows the clues and figures out the secret messages to solve a mystery. Grades 1–2.

Roy, Ron. *The Absent Author*. New York: Random, 1997. 86 p. Josh's favorite author is coming to his school, but when Wallace disappears, Josh suspects foul play. Grades 3–6.

_____. *The Missing Mummy*. New York: Random, 2001. 83 p. A mummy is stolen from the museum and Josh and his friends unravel the mystery to get the mummy back in its tomb. Grades 3–6.

_____. *The Talking T-Rex*. New York: Random, 2003. 96 p. Money being raised for a museum exhibit disappears and Dink, Josh, and Ruth Rose have to track down the cash. Grades 3–6.

Rumford, James. *Seeker of Knowledge: The Man Who Deciphered Egyptian Hieroglyphs*. Boston, MA: Houghton Mifflin, 2000. 32 p. Jean-Francois Champollion was the first modern person to uncover the secrets of hieroglyphics. Grades K–3.

Rushford, Patricia H. *Silent Witness*. Minneapolis, MN: Bethany House, 1993. 175 p. A bomb threat delays Jennie's trip to a dolphin research lab, but she gets to help solve a two-year-old murder case. Grades 6–8.

_____. *Too Many Secrets*. Minneapolis, MN: Bethany House, 1993. 172 p. Jennie's summer seems perfect until her grandmother disappears with a fortune in stolen jewels. Grades 6–8.

Russell, Joan Plummer. *Aero and Officer Mike: Police Partners*. Honesdale, PA: Boyds Mills, 2001. 32 p. A real-life Officer Buckle and Gloria duo, the work of Officer Mike and his K-9 companion is shown with color photographs. Grades K–2.

Ryan, Mary Elizabeth. *Alias*. New York: Pocket Book, 1998. 160 p. Toby has put up with constantly moving for more than a decade, but when he finally decides he wants to stay in one place, he discovers his mother's terrible secret. Grades 6–10.

Rylant, Cynthia. *The High-Rise Private Eye: The Case of the Missing Monkey*. New York: Greenwillow, 2001. 48 p. The High-Rise Private Eyes help the owner of a local diner find a missing glass monkey. Grades 1–3.

_____. *The High-Rise Private Eye: The Case of the Puzzling Possum*. New York: Greenwillow, 2001. 48 p. Bunny Brown and Jack Jones team up to crack cases wide open. In Case #003, Mr. Riley's trombone keeps disappearing and re-appearing. Grades 1–3.

Sachar, Louis. *Holes*. New York: Yearling, 2000. 233 p. Sent to a juvenile detention camp for a crime he didn't commit, Stanley Yelnats realizes that there is more to the punishment than the boys are being told. Grades 4–7.

Schaller, Bob. *Adventure in Wyoming: X Country Adventures*. Grand Rapids, MI: Baker Book, 2000. 127 p. Ashley and Adam Arlington travel around the country with their parents and they find mystery and adventure in every state. Grades 3–6.

Scheffler, Ursel. *The Spy in the Attic*. New York: North South, 1998. 64 p. After seeing people moving boxes into his new neighbor's apartment in the middle of the night, Martin fears that Mr. Leon is a foreign spy. Grades 2–4.

Schulman, Arlene. *Cop on the Beat: Officer Steven Mayfield in New York*. New York: Putnam, 2002. 144 p. Readers follow a New York City police officer as he works his beat. Includes a history of the police department. Grades 6–9.

Scieszka, Jon. *The Not-So-Jolly Roger*. New York: Penguin, 1993. 57 p. The Time-Warp Trio go back to the time of Blackbeard and witness the pirate's brutality. Grades 2–4.

Sebestyen, Ouida. *The Girl in the Box*. New York: Random, 2000. 182 p. Kidnapped and left in an underground box, Jackie writes letters to her parents and her captor. Her desperation mounts as she wonders whether she will ever be set free. Grades 5–7.

Sharmat, Marjorie Weinman. *Nate the Great*. New York: Delacorte, 2002. 65 p. The neighborhood "Sam Spade" solves cases and tracks down culprits. First in the series. Grades 1–2.
_____. *Nate the Great and the Crunchy Christmas*. New York: Bantam, 1997. 41 p. The junior sleuth and his canine sidekick solve the problem of missing holiday mail. Grades 1–3.
_____. *Nate the Great and Me: The Case of the Fleeing Fang*. New York: Yearling, 2000. 64 p. An empty chair at his Detective Day party provides a challenging mystery for Nate's guests. Grades 1–3.

Sharth, Sharon. *Way to Go!: Finding Your Way with a Compass*. Pleasantville, NY: Readers Digest, 2000. 48 p. Learn how a compass works and how to use it to find your way, as well as how to read a map. Grades 3–6.

Shaw, Murray. *Match Wits with Sherlock Holmes: The Adventures of the Dancing Men*. Minneapolis, MN: Lerner, 1993. 47 p. Abridgements of two Holmes stories stay true to the originals while providing an explanation of the clues and Holmes' reasoning. Grades 2–5.

Silverstein, Herma. *Kids Who Kill*. Brookfield, CT: Twenty-First Century Books, 1997. 128 p. With disturbing detail and accuracy, this book examines the causes and social impact of juvenile violence. Looks at actual cases of young people who murdered. Grades 10–12.

Simon, Seymour. *The Mysterious Lights and Other Cases*. New York: Morrow, 1998. 96 p. The 12-year-old whiz kid, Einstein Anderson, uses science to solve 10 puzzles. Grades 3–6.

Singh, Simon. *The Code Book: How to Make It, Break It, Hack It, Crack It.* New York: Bantam, 2002. 272 p. The history of cryptography and some of the famous people who have been involved in codes and codebreaking are explored. Grades 5–8.

Skofield, James. *Detective Dinosaur Lost and Found.* New York: Harper, 1999. 46 p. Detective Dinosaur and Officer Pterodactyl are comically clueless as the prehistoric duo try to solve problems with hilarious results. Grades K–2.

Skurzynski, Gloria and Alane Ferguson. *Deadly Waters.* Washington, D.C.: National Geographic, 1999. 160 p. The Landon kids uncover the mystery of dying manatees when they visit Everglades National Park. Grades 4–6.
_____. *Over the Edge.* Washington, D.C.: National Geographic, 2002. 149 p. California Condors are being poisoned in the Grand Canyon. Wildlife biologist Olivia Landon and her kids get involved in the search for the source of the poison. Grades 4–6.
_____. *Wolf Stalker.* Washington, D.C.: National Geographic, 2001. 149 p. The first title in the National Parks series combines science and survival skills at Yellowstone Park, as the Landon kids try to figure out who has shot a wolf. Grades 4–6.

Snicket, Lemony. *The Bad Beginning: Book the First.* New York: Harper, 1999. 176 p. Three unlucky siblings face unfortunate situations as they try to survive their ruthless and conniving relatives long enough to inherit their fortune. Grades 5–7.
_____. *Lemony Snicket: the Unauthorized Autobiography.* New York: Harper, 2002. 240 p. Peek into the mysterious life of a mysterious man to learn the tragic truth about the infamous Lemony Snicket. Grades 4–7.

Snyder, Zilpha Keatley. *Janie's Private Eye.* New York: Random, 1998. 212 p. Eight-year-old Janie starts her own detective agency after dogs start disappearing in her neighborhood. Grades 3–6.
_____. *The Egypt Game.* New York: Bantam, 1985. 240 p. Melanie and April stumble on a fantasy game that recreates Ancient Egypt. Grades 4–7.

Sobol, Donald. *Encyclopedia Brown and the Case of the Treasure Hunt.* New York: Bantam, 1988. 91 p. Ten more mysteries challenge the 10-year-old detective. Grades 3–6.
_____. *Encyclopedia Brown, Boy Detective.* New York: Bantam, 1978. 111 p. Ten mysteries challenge the boy detective as he uses his encyclopedic memory and investigative skills to solve crimes. Grades 3–6.

Stanley, Diane. *The Mysterious Matter of I. M. Fine.* New York: Harper, 2002. 208 p. The evil creations from a horror writer's books are coming to life so Franny and her friends set out to find the mysterious author and stop the mayhem. Grades 3–6.

Stanley, George Edward. *Adam Sharp: London Calling.* New York: Random, 2002. 44 p. Someone has stolen Big Ben and Adam Sharp is called to London to find the culprit. Grades K–2.
_____. *The Cobweb Confession.* New York: Aladdin, 2001. 80 p. A spider's web helps the third-grade detectives catch the person who stole a valuable baseball card collection. Grades 2–5.

Steffens, Bradley. *The Trial of Charles Manson: California Cult Murders.* San Diego, CA: Lucent, 2002. 112 p. A detailed account of the trials of Charles Manson and his followers provides an examination of the criminal justice system. Grades 9–12.

Stevenson, James. *Mud Flat Mystery.* New York: Harper, 2003. 64 p. A special-delivery box has all of the neighbors curious about its contents. Suspense mounts as they investigate. Grades 1–3.

Stevenson, Robert Louis. *Treasure Island.* New York: Signet, 1998. 224 p. Long John Silver and Jim Hawkins became part of our literary lore because of this swashbuckling adventure. Various editions available. Grades 5–12.

Stine, R.L. *The Haunting Hour: Chills in the Dead of Night.* New York: Harper, 2001. 160 p. The master of horror for children shares 10 tales of terror accompanied by illustrations by a variety of artists. Grades 3–6.

Stolz, Mary. *Casebook of a Private (Cat's) Eye.* Asheville, NC: Front Street, 1999. 128 p. Among the many crimes that Boston's only female feline detective has to solve is the case of a murdered chef and the theft of a valuable cookbook. Grades 4–6.

Tashijian, Janet. *Marty Frye, Private Eye.* New York: Little Apple, 2000. 80 p. Marty is a poet detective who makes up rhymes to solve the crimes. Grades 1–4.

Tate, Eleanora. *Minstrel's Melody.* Middleton, WI: Pleasant Co., 2001. 163 p. Orphelia meets a mysterious man and discovers a secret about her family's past when she runs away with a minstrel show. Grades 3–6.
_____. *The Secret of Gumbo Grove.* New York: Laurel Leaf, 1997. 208 p. Eleven-year-old Raisin solves a community mystery and gains pride in her family's past after helping to clean up an old cemetery. Grades 3–6

Titus, Eve. *Basil of Baker Street.* New York: Pocket Book, 1989. 95 p. Working with Sherlock Holmes, the great mouse detective solves the case of missing mouse twins. Grades 1–4.
_____. *Basil in the Wild West.* New York: Minstrel, 1990. 95 p. Basil is on the trail of a sinister smuggler and a ruthless mouse outlaw in the wild West. Grades 1–4.

Tolan, Stephanie. *Flight of the Raven.* New York: Harper, 2001. 304 p. Forced to flee into the wilderness after her father's involvement in a terrorist act puts the family in danger, Amber has to care for a young boy who has run away from a mental institution. Grades 7–10.
_____. *The Face in the Mirror.* New York: Harper, 2000. 214 p. Information about theater and acting are woven into this suspenseful tale as a 19th century ghost makes the stage a dangerous place. Grades 6–9.

Tryon, Leslie. *Albert's Halloween.* New York: Atheneum, 1998. 40 p. Detectives Miss Maple, Sharock Homes, Sam Slade, and Chief Inspector Albert join forces to find 18 missing pumpkins. Preschool–1.

Tudor, Tasha. *The Great Corgiville Kidnapping.* New York: Little Brown, 1999. 48 p. Caleb Corgi turns detective when "the biggest rooster on earth" is kidnapped. Preschool–2.

Ungerer, Tomi. *Crictor.* New York: Harper, 1984. 32 p. A boa constrictor saves the day when a burglar breaks into the house. Preschool–2.

Van Draanen, Wendelin. *Sammy Keyes and the Curse of Moustache Mary.* New York: Knopf, 1999. 208 p. Sammy spends the weekend with a friend and becomes involved in a mystery that dates back to the Hatfield-McCoy feud and buried treasure. Grades 5–8.
_____. *Sammy Keyes and the Hotel Thief.* New York: Random, 1998. 163 p. While killing time by spying on her neighbors, Sammy observes a thief stealing something, but the thief also sees Sammy and her life is now in danger. Grades 5–8.

Van Leeuwen, Jean. *The Great Googlestein Museum Mystery.* New York: Phyllis Fogelman, 2003. 208 p. Three mice, introduced in *The Great Christmas Kidnapping Caper*, leave the comfort of Macy's Department Store and find themselves involved in a mystery at the Guggenheim Museum. Grades 3–6.

Van Nutt, Julia. *The Mystery of Mineral Gorge.* New York: Bantam, 1999. 32 p. Lucky Hart chronicles life in a 19th century town as she joins a search party to identify the source of a haunting scream coming from Mineral Gorge. Grades 2–5.

Velde, Vivian Vande. *There's a Dead Person Following My Sister Around.* San Diego, CA: Harcourt, 1999. 143 p. Ted discovers that there are things worse than homework and school—like ghosts! And one is following his sister around the house. Grades 4–7.

Voigt, Cynthia. *The Callender Papers.* New York: Aladdin, 2000. 224 p. Hired to sort and catalog some papers, Jean moves into the old Callender House for the summer. There she discovers an unsolved mystery than may put her life in danger. Grades 5–7.

Wallace, Barbara Brooks. *Secret in St. Something.* New York: Simon & Schuster, 2001. 160 p. The bleak streets of New York in the late 19th century are dangerous for two runaway kids. Grades 5–7.

Walsh, Ellen Stoll. *Dot & Jabber and the Great Acorn Mystery*. San Diego, CA: Harcourt, 2001. 40 p. Two mouse detectives investigate a lone oak tree to figure out how it got so far away from the rest of the trees. Preschool–1.
_____. *Dot & Jabber and the Mystery of the Missing Stream.* San Diego, CA: Harcourt, 2002. 40 p. After a rainstorm, the stream is empty, so the mouse detectives investigate to find out where the water went. Preschool–1.

Warner, Gertrude Chandler. *The Panther Mystery.* Morton Grove, IL: Whitman, 1998. 128 p. A ranger in the Everglades is missing and the Boxcar children think his interest in panthers may have played a part in his disappearance. Grades 3–6.
_____. *The Summer Camp Mystery.* Morton Grove, IL: Whitman, 2001. 128 p. The Boxcar children do not experience the same joy that their grandfather did at camp, especially when their belongings start to disappear. Grades 3–6.

Watson, M.D., John H. *The Quotable Sherlock Holmes*. New York: Mysterious Press, 2000. 233 p. The wit, wisdom, and philosophy of Sherlock Holmes is found through this compilation of notable quotations. Grades 9–Adult.

Weill, Sabrina Solin. *We're Not Monsters: Teens Speak Out about Teens in Trouble*. New York: Harper, 2002. 240 p. Issues, facts, statistics, and advice are candidly explored through the voices of teenagers, some of whom have made the news because of their actions. Grades 8–12.

Wells, Rosemary. *The Man in the Woods*. New York: Puffin, 2000. 231 p. After Helen witnesses a hit-and-run accident, she follows the perpetrator into the woods. When the police arrest the wrong person, the man stalks her. Grades 5–8.

Werlin, Nancy. *The Killer's Cousin*. New York: Laurel Leaf, 2000. 240 p. David Yaffe was acquitted of murder in the death of his girlfriend, but he has to cope with questions and uncertainty from his family, friends, and neighbors. Grades 7–10.
_____. *Locked Inside*. New York: Laurel Leaf, 2001. 272 p. The wealthy daughter of a super-star who was killed in a plane crash, 16-year-old Marnie meets a mysterious boy in an Internet game room. Kidnapped and locked away, Marnie faces many painful truths. Grades 7–10.

Whatley, Bruce and Rosie Smith. *Detective Donut and the Wild Goose Chase*. New York: Harper, 1999. 32 p. Detective Duck's friend is missing and he has to find the professor and his Maltese statue before the notorious goose thief can. Preschool–2.

White, Graham. *Secrets of the Pyramids: a Maze Adventure*. Washington, D.C.: National Geographic, 2002. 32 p. Hemon needs help finding his father, an explorer who is lost in the maze of an Egyptian pyramid. Grades 3–6.

Whitney, Phyllis. *The Mystery of the Haunted Pool*. Philadelphia: Westminster, 1960. 224 p. (Out of print.) Susan Price and her aunt stay in the mysterious house they rent from Captain Dan, but strange things keep happening and when an ominous face appears in the pool, Susan is frightened. Grades 6–8.

William, Stanley "Tookie." *Life in Prison*. New York: SeaStar, 2001. 80 p. The co-founder of the Crips gang and a death-row inmate was nominated for the Nobel Peace Prize for his anti-gang efforts. He offers advice to help kids make better choices than he did. Grades 3–8.

Wilson, Eric. *Vancouver Nightmare: a Tom Austen Mystery*. Victoria, BC: Orca, 2000. 112 p. Dirty dealings are keeping Tom Austen busy in this Canadian mystery series. Grades 4–7.

Winterfeld, Henry. *Detectives in Togas*. San Diego, CA: Odyssey Classics, 2002. 272 p. Three young Romans find their teacher bound and gagged and a boy is wrongly accused of several crimes. Grades 5–8.

Winters, Paul A. *Crime*. San Diego, CA: Greenhaven, 1998. 144 p. Part of the Current Controversies series, short essays explore the many issues related to crime in the United States. Grades 6–10.

Wisniewski, David. *The Secret Knowledge of Grown-Ups: The Second File.* New York: Harper, 2001. 48 p. The secrets behind parental rules and the conspiracy of adult reasoning are explored with comical results in this dossier. Grades 2–6.

_____. *Tough Cookie.* New York: Lothrop, 1999. 48 p. Tough Cookie, a detective, prepares to bring a kidnapper to justice. Grades 1–3.

Wright, Betty Ren. *Christina's Ghost.* New York: Scholastic, 1995. 128 p. Spending the summer with her uncle in a creepy old house, Christina hears strange noises and sees the ghost of a boy. Grades 3–6.

_____. *The Dollhouse Murders.* New York: Scholastic, 1995. 174 p. Danger lurks in every corner of a mysterious dollhouse. Grades 4–6.

_____. *The Moonlight Man.* New York: Scholastic, 2000. 181 p. Fifteen-year-old Jenny has moved more times than she can remember, so she is determined not to let mysterious sounds and visions scare her away. Grades 4–7.

_____. *Pet Detectives.* Troll, 2000. 32 p. Kitty, a cat, and Belle, a dog, team up to help Policeman Jack when a burglar breaks into his house in this clever tale told all in verse. Preschool–2.

Yee, Wong Herbert. *The Officers' Ball.* Boston, MA: Houghton Mifflin, 1997. 32 p. Sgt. Hippo takes dancing lessons to prepare for the Policeman's Ball, but his lessons are cut short by the demands of crime-solving. Preschool–2

Yep, Laurence. *The Case of the Goblin Pearls.* New York: Harper, 1998. 179 p. A set of valuable pearls is stolen during the Chinatown parade, and 12-year-old Lily and her auntie Tiger Lil trace the thieves. Grades 4–7.

_____. *The Mark Twain Murders.* New York: Four Winds, 1982. 152 p. After a murder has occurred, a teenage boy meets Mark Twain and agrees to help the San Francisco reporter get the story. Grades 3–7.

Yolen, Jane. *Ballad of the Pirate Queens.* San Diego, CA: Voyager, 1998. 32 p. The lives of Anne Bonney and Mary Reade, real-life women pirates, are recounted in a picture book for older readers with illustrations by David Shannon. Grades 3–6.

_____. *The Emperor and the Kite.* Paper Star, 1998. 32 p. When the Emperor is imprisoned in a high tower only the princess knows how to save him. Preschool–2.

_____. *Picnic with Piggins.* San Diego, CA: Voyager, 1993. 32 p. One of the Reynard kits disappears and Piggins has to follow the clues to unravel the mystery. Preschool–2.

_____. *Piggins.* San Diego, CA: Voyager, 1992. 32 p. Piggins, the butler, finds Mrs. Reynard's missing diamonds. Preschool–2.

Zindel, Paul. *Scream Museum.* New York: Hyperion, 2001. 149 p. P.C. Hawke is shocked to learn that his friend, a custodian at the Museum of Natural History, has been accused of murder. With his friend Mackenzie Riggs, he sets out to prove his friend's innocence. Grades 4–7.

Works Cited and Further Reading

The American Psychiatric Association. *Psychiatric Effects of Media Violence.* 25 May 2003 <http://www.psych.org/public_info/media_violence.cfm>.

Anderson, Richard C. et al, *Becoming a Nation of Readers: The Report of the Commission on Reading* (Washington, D.C.: National Institute of Education, 1985).

Beers, Kylene G. Texas Library Association Conference. Dallas Convention Center. April 21–23, 1999.

Bell, A. Craig. "The Rise and Fall of the Detective Novel." *Contemporary Review.* 272 (1998) 197–201.

Billman, Carol. "The Child Reader as Sleuth." *Children's Literature in Education.* Spring 1984: 30–41.

Billman, Carol. *The Secret of the Stratemeyer Syndicate: Nancy Drew, the Hardy Boys, and the Million Dollar Fiction Factory.* New York: Ungar, 1986.

Cline, Ruth and William McBride. *A Guide to Literature for Young Adults.* Glenville, IL: Scott, Foresman and Co., 1983.

Cline, Ruth. "Detective Story." 2003 *Encyclopædia Britannica* Online. March 2, 2003 <http://search.eb.com/ebi/article?eu=295819>.

Flack, Jerry D. *Mystery and Detection: Thinking and Problem Solving with the Sleuths.* Englewood, CO: Teacher Ideas, 1990.

Flack, Jerry D. "Put Some Mystery in Your Classroom." *Teaching K–8,* 22:3. Nov/Dec 1991. 62–65.

Grunbaum, Jo Anne. *Youth Risk Behavior Surveillance—United States, 2001.* MMWR; June 21, 2002; 51(SS04); 1–64.

Howe, James. "Mirth & Mayhem: Humor and Mystery in Children's Books." Voices from the Middle, 2.3. 1995. 4–9.

Howe, James. "Writing Mysteries for Children." *The Horn Book.* 66 (1990) 178–183.

Huesmann, L. Rowell. "The Psychology of Media Violence: Why it Has a Lasting Impact on Children." 25 May 2003 <http://www.extension.iastate.edu/families/media/qa.huesmann.html>.

Johnson, Deidre. *Edward Stratemeyer and the Stratemeyer Syndicate.* New York: Twayne, 1993.

Kellerman, Jonathan. *Savage Spawn: Reflections on Violent Children.* New York: Ballantine, 1999.

Kids & Media @ the New Millennium: A Comprehensive National Analysis of Children's Media Use. Menlo Park, CA: Kaiser Family Foundation. November 1999. 25 May 2003 <http://www.kff.org/content/1999/1535/>.

Larson, Jeanette. "Mysteries for Young Detectives." *Book Links.* 10.1 (2000) 57–61.

McFarlane, Leslie. *The Ghost of the Hardy Boys.* Toronto: Methuen, 1976.

Myers, Walter Dean. "Escalating Offenses." *The Horn Book.* 77 (2001) 701–2.

Mystery Writers of America. Advertisement. 1997.

Norton, Donna E. *Through the Eyes of a Child: an Introduction to Children's Literature.* 3rd ed. New York: Macmillan, 1991.

Prager, Arthur. "Edward Stratemeyer and his Book Machine." *Saturday Review of Literature,* July 10, 1971. 15–17+.

Roberts, Willo Davis. "Writing Mysteries for Young Readers." *The Writer.* May 1996: 21–3.

Saltman, Judith. "Groaning Under the Weight of Series Books." *Emergency Librarian.* 24 (1997): 23–25.

Steinbrunner, Chris and Otto Penzler, ed. *Encyclopedia of Mystery and Detection.* New York: McGraw-Hill, 1976.

Sugarman, Sally. "The Mysterious Case of the Detective as Child Hero." Annual Joint Meetings of the Popular Culture Association/American Culture Association. Philadelphia. 12–15 April 1995.

Trelease, Jim. *The Read-Aloud Handbook.* 4th ed. New York: Penguin, 1995.

Tunnell, Michael O. "Books in the Classroom: Mysteries." *The Horn Book.* 66 (1990) 242–244.

U.S. Departments of Education and Justice. *Indicators of School Crime and Safety, 2002.* 25 May 2003. <http://www.ojp.usdoj.gov/bjs/abstract/iscs02.htm>.

Index of Subjects